Total Instructional Alignment

From Standards to Student Success

Lisa Carter

Foreword by Dr. Lawrence W. Lezotte

Solution Tree | Press

a division of

Solution Tree

555 North Morton Street
Bloomington, IN 47404
800.733.6786 (toll free) / 812.336.7700
FAX: 812.336.7790

email: info@solution-tree.com
solution-tree.com

Cover design by Grannan Graphic Design, Ltd.

Printed in the United States of America

10   09   4   5

FSC
Mixed Sources
Product group from well-managed
forests and other controlled sources
Cert no. SW-COC-002283
www.fsc.org
© 1996 Forest Stewardship Council

ISBN: 978-1-934009-01-7

Dedication

To Derb S. Carter

In gratitude to a father who taught me strength, conviction, and the value of education.

Acknowledgements

There simply is not enough room to list the names of all the individuals who deserve to be recognized in these acknowledgements. There are so many people—family, friends, and respected professional colleagues—who have made such a significant difference in my life and my life's work. I will forever be grateful.

It is important, however, for me to take this special opportunity to recognize by name some individuals who provided me with tremendous support and have had a powerful and positive influence on both my personal and professional growth.

Dr. Lawrence Lezotte and Dr. Ruth Lezotte have served as inspirations and continue to support me in so many ways.

Dr. Larry Rowedder, a former superintendent, continued friend, and mentor, taught me how to be a principal and opened many doors of opportunity for me that I never even knew existed.

Toni Moynihan-McKoy, a teacher and friend, helped me to understand early on the importance of instructional alignment and its impact on student learning.

Mr. Dennis Monroe, a colleague and friend, has permitted me to share his story of hope wherever I go to illustrate the power of Total Instructional Alignment.

The faculty and staff of the Mayerson Academy for Human Resource Development in Cincinnati, Ohio, provided me with the opportunity to learn, grow, and develop as a presenter, consultant, and teacher.

The staff of Learning 24/7 has allowed me so many opportunities to share ideas with thousands of educators all across the country.

My family—Dad, Drew, Rebecca, Yancey, Derb, Ann, and my husband, Mike—who gave me their unconditional love, support, and encouragement each and every day.

Finally, it goes without saying that this book would have been impossible without the thousands of dedicated teachers and administrators who work hard every day to put the foundations of Total Instructional Alignment into practice. You are truly the heroes.

Table of Contents

About the Author

Lisa Carter, Ed.S., received her baccalaureate in early childhood education, masters degrees in early childhood education and school administration, and an educational specialist degree in school administration, all from East Carolina University. Lisa began her career as an elementary school teacher in Fayetteville, North Carolina. She has served as an administrator at both the elementary and secondary levels and has worked in rural and urban schools. Lisa helped to establish and served as executive director for the Mayerson Academy for Human Resource Development in Cincinnati, Ohio, recognized for its outstanding work in the professional development of teachers and administrators. She is a noted presenter, keynote speaker, author, and consultant.

Foreword

The foreword to a book should seek to accomplish two goals. First, it should place the book in a larger context in hopes that the reader will read it with this larger problem or issue in mind. Second, it should persuade the prospective reader of the importance of the text. In other words, it should say why he or she should read the book. I was honored when asked to prepare a foreword to this manuscript, and I set out to do so with these goals in mind. After I read the manuscript, I found myself facing a dilemma.

Total Instructional Alignment: From Standards to Student Success addresses one of the basic cornerstones of school improvement: instructional alignment of standards, curriculum, instruction, and assessment. Therefore, little effort is needed to make the case as to how this book fits into the larger context of educational reform today. Whether a professional educator or a concerned parent or citizen, anyone familiar with the accountability and standards movement of the past 10 years or the sweeping educational reform legislation No Child Left Behind is keenly aware of the need to address the issue of instructional alignment in schools. Fortunately, this manuscript provides not a theory, but a clear, coherent, and compelling process by which the crucial tasks of alignment can be completed. It is a practical guide to an essential, but demanding, task.

Given the description of this excellent book, what then is my dilemma? The author openly discusses one of the best-kept secrets in American education: *Children tend to learn those things they are taught.* This is the dilemma. How many educational consultants, educational material developers, and supplemental service providers would be put out of business if every teacher and principal knew this secret? Maybe it would be in the best interest of educational reformers like myself if practitioners did *not* read this book and implement the alignment system it advocates. But while keeping this alignment process a secret may be beneficial for many adults, it is clearly not in the best interest of students. How are children's interests served if they are tested on the basis of standards they have not been taught? For me, the dilemma is resolved. I advise all educators and administrators to read the book and implement the system.

School reform is and always will be first a moral journey. Those who believe that school change simply represents a technical adjustment in school practices just do not get it. Learning for all—leaving no child behind—is at the core of our democracy. Instructional alignment that assures all children have an opportunity to learn is fundamental to success on this moral journey. We know that when students are tested on things they have not been taught, they pay the price for this adult negligence. And it is the neediest students who pay the greatest price. How can any educational leader stand by and watch as the students who are most dependent on the school as their source of academic learning are shortchanged by the system?

Total Instructional Alignment is a prerequisite to school effectiveness. Students have a right to be taught the curricular standards on which they will be assessed. In addition, any other innovation that a school adopts to improve results on student assessments presumes that there is tight alignment between the intended, taught, and tested curricula.

Total Instructional Alignment should be the first priority on the endless journey to sustainable school reform. Those adults—the consultants and presenters like me—who will be inconvenienced if teachers and building leaders discover the Total Instructional

Alignment process will have to find other ways to help schools advance the moral journey of learning for all.

—Dr. Lawrence W. Lezotte, author, consultant, educator, researcher, and founder of Effective Schools Products, Ltd.

Introduction

The No Child Left Behind Act presents a unique challenge for educators. It requires that all schools deliver what public education promised when it was founded more than a century ago: education for all. But is it truly possible for schools to ensure that all students learn, and learn well, those things they are expected to master? For years, educators have struggled to design such a system; and yet, no matter how hard we tried, there were always students we were not able to reach, students who slipped through the cracks. Much to our dismay, many of these students continued to be passed through the system year after year, falling farther and farther behind.

Because of this intractable failure, a law now requires us to not only teach, but also to reach every student and ensure that he or she learns. With so many unsuccessful reform efforts coming and going in our schools, many principals and teachers have become disillusioned. It can be painful to consider making yet another change. Despite all the programs and innovations designed to fix our schools and improve student achievement, there is one basic question that has often gone unasked: Are students actually being *taught* those things we expect them to learn?

According to one study, more than 58% of the teachers surveyed indicated they did not feel they received much guidance about what to teach from state standards, and more than half of the teachers surveyed said that state and school district guidelines have not led them to expect more from their students ("New Standards," 2000).

By design, standards are often stated in vague or broad terms, leaving them open to a wide range of individual interpretations. Although many states have taken further steps to define specific learning expectations through the development of benchmarks and specific grade-level or course content, these too are often ambiguous, repetitious, and up to the individual interpretation of teachers. As a result, each year millions of students sit down to grueling high-stakes tests that can determine their fate in school—and their school's fate as well—with no real assurance that they have been taught the material on which they are being assessed.

It is helpful to see this problem from a student's perspective. Let us pretend I am the teacher and you are the student. I have chosen a short lesson to teach you some important information about dogs. I have decided to focus on a specific breed of dog, the Labrador retriever, because I have some knowledge and experience from having owned one for many years.

The Dog Lesson

Now, I realize some of you may already have had some experience with Labrador retrievers; they are a very popular breed of dog. However, if you have never owned one and you are considering keeping a Labrador retriever as a pet, there are some important things to keep in mind before you make your final decision.

1. Labrador Retrievers come in three basic colors: black, yellow, and chocolate. These colors are always solid. Therefore, if you encounter a big black dog that closely resembles a Labrador retriever, but has a white spot on his chest, you will know it is not a purebred dog.

2. Labrador retrievers may start out as cute little puppies, but they quickly grow up into great big dogs. Females can weigh between 65 and 75 pounds, and males can weigh 75 to 85 pounds. Some Labrador retrievers have been known to

weigh more than 100 pounds! Owning a dog this size is much like owning a small horse. There are many things to consider if you are interested in owning a large dog. Do you have the space? Do you have the time? Do you have a lot of valuable items on low coffee tables?

3. At dog shows, Labrador retrievers are in the sporting class division. They have all the characteristics of active hunting dogs: They are excellent swimmers, retrieve effortlessly, have keen senses and great strength, and are very intelligent. They are also obedient. They are very aware of their surroundings, and their keen senses make them an excellent choice as guide dogs and detectors of illegal drugs. Because they are so obedient, you will see as many Labrador retrievers in the obedience ring at dog shows as you will in the conformation ring.

4. Most Labrador retrievers have very sweet dispositions. Their nature is to please people, and they do not discriminate. They love everyone! So, if you want a guard dog for protection, a Labrador retriever might not be your first choice. At best, a Labrador retriever might lick an intruder to death!

The Dog Test

Now that you have experienced the dog lesson, it is time to take the dog test. How well will you do based on what you have learned?

(continued)

The Dog Test

1. Draw two show-ring patterns a judge may ask a dog handler to use during conformation judging.

2. Distinguish between obedience and conformation in dog judging.

3. What color puppies are possible when a black Labrador retriever is bred to a yellow Labrador retriever?

4. True or false: Labrador retrievers are considered working class dogs.

5. Name four class divisions a dog can be entered in during conformation judging.

6. Why do Labrador retriever owners need big backyards?

7. A Labrador retriever must accumulate 15 points to become a champion. How many of these points must be accumulated at major shows?

8. Describe what it means when a dog is entered as a "Special" during competition.

9. What does the competition title "Best of Breed" mean?

10. List three characteristics of a good hunting dog.

(When you are finished, turn to page 18 to find the answers.)

So, how did you do? Did you find you were unable to answer a few of the questions? In fact, if you are like most people, you found this test rather frustrating. Only two of the answers could be drawn directly from the lesson: the Labrador retriever's dog-show class and the characteristics of hunting dogs. You might have inferred the answer to question six from the discussion of the dog's size. Perhaps you answered some questions correctly because you have had prior experience with Labrador retrievers or dog shows. Or you may have just gotten lucky. For example, you had a 50/50 chance of guessing the correct answer to question four. If you got a passing grade on the dog test, you did not have the dog lesson to thank for it.

You have just experienced what happens to many students when they are in a misaligned instructional program. The question is not whether you could have learned the information on which you were being assessed. Of course you could have. The question is, *were you taught* the information? This is often the case with our students; their poor performance on student assessments is not a result of an inability to learn. All students can learn; however, they can only learn those things they are taught.

It is interesting to observe how administrators and teachers react to the dog lesson and test in my training sessions. As you might expect, they usually complain about how unfair the whole experience is, and say it is not their fault that they got failing grades. Why did I not teach them those things for which I was holding them accountable? I respond with some familiar excuses to their complaints about the missing content in the lesson: I ran out of time. It was content they should have learned last year, so it wasn't my responsibility to teach it. Sometimes I tell them the content wasn't in the textbook or the materials I was given to use as a resource. Or, worst of all, the reason I didn't teach it was because I don't particularly like it. But whatever the reason, the participants quickly realize there was a serious disconnect between the dog lesson and the dog test—a disconnect over which they had no control.

Often, they want to talk about the information in the lesson that never showed up on the test. They readily admit that some of this extra information was the most interesting. They often remark about how well I taught the lesson. One teacher told me, "You did a great job teaching us all the wrong information!" But the information was not wrong; it simply was not aligned to the assessment I was using to measure achievement.

Sometimes, the effect of prior knowledge is evident in someone's score on the dog test. Believe it or not, people have received a perfect score on the test, despite the fact that they heard the same lesson and took the same test as everyone else. How did they do it? One such person was a third-grade teacher in Cincinnati. The rest of the class was in a state of disbelief until she revealed that, on her weekends, she was also a judge for the American Kennel Association. She knew the answers before the lesson began. We know there are students who also bring the required information to the assessment from outside the classroom. These fortunate students have access to resources that enable them to learn the kinds of things we assess in our schools. They do well on assessments even if we do not present the information in our instructional program.

The final element of frustration comes when I use participants' dog test scores to place them in compensatory programs. For example, anyone scoring between 50 and 65 qualifies for remedial services. Anyone scoring below 50 is referred for additional testing for a suspected learning disability. The Ohio third-grade teacher who got a perfect score made it into the academically gifted program. With this, participants' frustration turns to anger. They indicate that it would be grossly unfair to label them as in need of remedial services or learning disabled based on a test score when they were never given the opportunity to learn the tested information. I always respond, "Why not?" After all, for years we have placed students in these programs using standardized test scores that are not aligned to any particular curriculum.

At this point in the demonstration, I see the realization in the faces of many educators. No school reform effort we undertake—from technology to smaller classes, from professional development to increased testing—can succeed without instructional alignment. In the era of educational accountability, we simply cannot afford to keep giving our kids the dog test.

Common Alignment Myths

As I work with schools and school districts throughout the country, I have developed a deep admiration for the tremendous devotion and spirit of teachers and administrators. If misalignment exists, it is not a result of a lack of hard work and dedication on behalf of educators. It is due mostly to a lack of understanding of the alignment process and the basic nature of school improvement. I have encountered many common misconceptions about instructional alignment. These misconceptions are so prevalent that I refer to them as common alignment myths. These myths must be overcome if schools and districts are to move forward in the alignment process.

Myth 1: If we wait, the crisis will surely go away.

This myth exists mainly because educators have seen so many school reform movements come and go; but the public demand for accountability in education is here to stay. Schools will be held increasingly accountable for ensuring that all students learn and for demonstrating this learning through results on student assessments. For many years, almost no accountability existed for student achievement in our schools. Student failure seemed to yield few consequences for the school or school district. Over the past decade, however, most states have developed content standards and assessments with strong accountability measures based on student performance. These measures can vary greatly from state to state, but they are all designed for the same purpose: to hold schools and school districts accountable for increasing student achievement. No

Child Left Behind now makes accountability the law nationwide. Educators who think they can wait out the accountability movement do so at their peril.

Myth 2: We can continue to use the same old delivery methods to help students meet or exceed rigorous standards.

The delivery methods of the past simply have not yielded the desired results. This is evidenced by the continuing national focus on the need to close the achievement gap between advantaged and disadvantaged students. According to the National Center for Educational Statistics, minority students on average score lower than white students in reading and math. Similar gaps exist between students based on income levels and immigration patterns (Jacobson, Olsen, Rice, Sweetland, & Ralph, 2001). The old educational delivery system was never designed to educate all students.

One example of the inadequacy of the old system is the way it deals with the varying knowledge and skill levels of students. We know that students learn at different rates and that learning, for the most part, is an incremental process. However, the design of the current educational system is to hold time as a *constant.* In other words, all students are given the same amount of time to learn the same amount of content. When time to learn is held as a *constant,* learning itself becomes a *variable.* If we are truly going to ensure that all students meet or exceed learning expectations, our school systems will have to be redesigned to make learning the constant, which means that time to learn will have to vary with the needs of each student.

Myth 3: Instructional alignment is simply "teaching the test."

This is one of the most common myths about alignment. There is often confusion about the difference between "teaching the test" and "teaching to the tested concepts" (also known as "teaching to the test"). Teaching the test involves having some idea of what the test questions will be and teaching the answers to students. This method does not promote learning, and it is downright dishonest and could be considered cheating. Teaching to the tested concepts, on the other hand, involves understanding which concepts will be assessed and teaching those concepts to students. Then, no matter what questions are asked, students can apply their knowledge of the concepts to answer the questions. Teaching to assessed concepts is the teacher's moral and ethical obligation.

Although it is only logical to teach those concepts we will ultimately assess, remember that instructional alignment is much more comprehensive. It involves alignment of the system; alignment of standards, curriculum, and assessments; and, most importantly, alignment of instructional practices in the classroom.

Myth 4: Standards and assessments stifle teacher creativity.

Creativity is still a very important part of the alignment process. Standards and benchmarks define the parameters of what we want students to know and be able to do; assessments define how we will know they have learned. Once a teacher has a clear understanding of what students are expected to learn and how that learning will be assessed, he or she must develop lessons to teach those important concepts to students. Individual creativity allows each teacher to find exciting and motivational ways to deliver instruction to students every day. We can probably remember a teacher whose creative efforts inspired us to learn. Creativity is often what instills in students the desire to learn. Obviously, if students are not motivated to learn, how well the instructional program is aligned will not matter. While what we teach is important, *how we teach* is just as crucial an element of instructional alignment.

Myth 5: Curriculum alignment and instructional alignment are synonymous.

Although the terms are often used interchangeably, "curriculum alignment" and "instructional alignment" are not one and the same. Curriculum alignment is the process many districts use to ensure that the taught curriculum is aligned to existing standards and assessments. This work is usually translated into a curriculum document teachers are expected to follow for their instruction throughout the year. Unfortunately, even the most well-developed curriculum documents often remain on shelves in classrooms, and seldom influence instructional practice. Therefore, simply aligning the curriculum does not guarantee that instruction is aligned.

Instructional alignment is a step beyond curriculum alignment. Obviously, curriculum alignment must first exist if we want teachers to align instruction in the classroom; however, instructional alignment has its ultimate impact on the teacher's behavior in the classroom.

Myth 6: Innovations by themselves will improve student performance.

It is simply amazing how much time, how many resources, and how much human energy are channeled each year into innovations that promise to be the answer to improved student achievement. Innovations, by themselves, will not improve student assessment results if alignment does not exist. If I attempted to improve student results on the dog test through an innovation, perhaps technology, I could write a grant to purchase everyone a laptop computer. Then, without changing anything else, I could teach the exact same lesson, only this time present it in an exciting interactive format using the laptops. If I then give the exact same test, this time on your computer, is it likely that your performance will be any better? Of course not! The laptop computer does not know how to fix my content errors.

While it is an extremely important tool in our instructional pro-grams, technology can only be effective if I teach those things I assess.

Myth 7: My textbook is my curriculum.

This myth is still alive and well in many schools and classrooms. With the onset of standards, benchmarks, and high-stakes assess-ments, the textbook can only be viewed as a valuable resource for the teacher. Few—if any—textbooks are totally congruent with a given curriculum. Despite the lack of congruence, however, many teachers still rely heavily on the textbook to deliver instruction in the classroom. I have heard from some teachers that more than half of the textbook they were issued at the beginning of the school year contained information that was incongruent to the standards they were expected to teach and the assessments they were giving their students. While a good textbook can be a useful tool, following an incongruent textbook page by page throughout the instructional process is a sure sign of a misaligned instructional program.

Myth 8: Give teachers the standards, and they will figure them out.

Teachers want to make sure their students are successful. Most teachers are doing the very best they can, given what they know. I was presenting to a group of 60 third-grade teachers. We were look-ing at their state standards as they began to develop curriculum maps for the upcoming school year. These teachers seemed per-plexed by an impressive-looking math standard in their standards document. After some discussion, I finally asked, "What does that standard mean, and how will you know when your students have successfully met the standard?" Their unanimous response was that they did not know what the standard meant. What, I asked, did they do when they got to that learning expectation in their curriculum? They collectively responded, "We skip it!"

For teachers to be successful in a standards-based program, they need tools, processes, and time to work collaboratively to align their instructional programs. It is very important that appropriate professional development, support, resources, and leadership be available in every school to assist them in this process.

The Need for Total Instructional Alignment

These myths infect the thinking of many educators; thus, there is a great need for a resource that defines instructional alignment properly, examines its importance, and helps schools implement a model that offers the greatest hope for the kind of improvements expected of educators in this era of accountability.

The purpose of this book is to present a comprehensive look at a process called Total Instructional Alignment (also known as TIA), and the impact of that process on student achievement. Leaving no child behind will require that all schools design an instructional program that not only aligns instruction to standards, benchmarks, and assessments, but also presents instruction that is aligned to the learning needs of each individual student. I call this process Total Instructional Alignment because it is more than just teaching those things we test; it affects all aspects of the educational program we design for our students.

About This Book

This book will help you move from general ideas to specific practice. **Chapter 1** presents a conceptual framework for understanding the Total Instructional Alignment process. This conceptual framework focuses on the three broad aspects of TIA: alignment of the system; alignment of standards, curriculum, and assessment; and alignment of instructional practices in the classroom.

Chapter 2 focuses on alignment of the system, a crucially important, but often overlooked, aspect of the TIA process. There is no question that the new mission of public schools—to ensure that all students meet or exceed the rigorous learning expectations set for them—will not be accomplished unless the system is redesigned to meet the individual learning needs of students. The old educational system, developed over a century ago, was never designed to meet the learning needs of *all* students. This chapter examines vertical and horizontal structures and flexible grouping practices, as well as the roles of policies, practices, and leadership in redesigning the educational system to ensure all students learn.

An important step in the alignment process is to make sure every classroom teacher has a clear understanding of the learning expectations for students. Therefore, **chapter 3** explores ways to align standards, benchmarks, curriculum, and assessments and present them clearly and specifically to the classroom teacher. This chapter will address what teachers are to teach. Chapter 3 will introduce the first important alignment tool—the congruence matrix—designed to help teachers collect and examine all that is to be taught and assessed.

Chapter 4 focuses on the alignment of instruction in the classroom. It matters little how well the curriculum is aligned to existing standards, benchmarks, and assessments if the curriculum is not implemented in the classroom. This chapter introduces the second critical alignment tool: standards-driven/objective-based instruction in the classroom. To fully align instruction in a standards-based program, teachers must develop clear learning goals in the form of good, solid behavioral objectives, including objectives that address higher levels of thinking. Another important alignment tool, task analysis, helps teachers take broad learning expectations and break them down into the specific essential learning necessary to accomplish the goal.

Chapter 5 explores the role of ongoing assessment in the alignment process. How do we know if our students are learning, and how well they are learning, those things we are teaching? The purpose of assessment should be to gain information about student progress that can be used to make adjustments in the instructional program. This can only be accomplished by setting standards for mastery and establishing proper assessment methods in the classroom. Since there are numerous ways to assess student learning, this chapter focuses on the purpose and use of multiple assessment instruments. It will also explore the importance of benchmark assessments designed to give teachers specific and immediate feedback about student progress during the instructional year. Chapter 5 also includes information on helping students prepare to take standardized assessments as an integral part of the instructional program.

Chapter 6 concludes the book with a look at sustainable reform. Educators often view school reform as LYNT, TYNT or NYNT: Last Year's New Thing, This Year's New Thing, or Next Year's New Thing. As a result, teachers and administrators sometimes become disillusioned with yet another school improvement initiative before it can even begin. This attitude can become a self-fulfilling prophecy, and many changes that occur in the name of school reform are often superficial and short-lived. Total Instructional Alignment is not another educational fad. It is an integral part of any effective instructional program. Chapter 6 will examine the necessary ingredients of meaningful change and how to bring about and sustain the TIA process.

The Dennis Monroe Story

One particular experience helped me to truly understand the power of Total Instructional Alignment in the classroom. Dennis Monroe was one of the most outstanding teachers with whom I have had the opportunity to work. Dennis' leadership ability later enabled him to become vice principal in a middle school, and he now serves as a principal. When I met him, Dennis was a sixth-grade teacher and taught all the science and health classes at the school where I was principal. I heard stories about Dennis before I even arrived. I heard that he was 6 foot 5 inches tall, which really stands out in an elementary school! He was motivational. The students loved him. The parents loved him. His fellow teachers admired and loved him as well.

After visiting classrooms the first 2 weeks of school, I realized I had the great opportunity to lead a new staff of outstanding teachers. I observed teachers who were prepared for class. They arrived early and they stayed late. Overall, they had great rapport with their students and few classroom-management problems. However, there was one thing that troubled me: It was obvious they were bound to textbooks as their main source of instruction.

From previous experience, I knew the textbooks used in the district were, at best, loosely aligned to our new standards and assessments. And if classroom instruction was to proceed page by page through the text, there was a great possibility students would be assessed on information they had not been taught. In an attempt to ensure that this did not happen, at the next staff meeting I gave each teacher a blank yearly course outline for the core areas of math, science, social studies, and language arts/communications.

Dennis had his science outline on my desk first thing the next morning. I was amazed at his speed, but when I examined the outline I realized how he had completed it so quickly. His week-1 learning goals were, "Introduction to Text, Content and Format." Week 2 goals were for students to "Read Chapter One: The Planet Earth." In week 3, the learning goals were chapter review, study guide, and quiz. The outline continued this way until week 36, which read, "Final Exam, Collect Textbooks."

I asked Dennis how much of the content of his science textbook aligned to the North Carolina State Standards and the sixth-grade science test given at the end of the year. He said, "I don't know, but I think a lot of it is." He explained that he thought it was aligned because his students usually averaged around the 53rd percentile on the state science test—above the state average. Those were pretty decent scores, considering we served a highly mobile population that included many poor and disadvantaged students. But how much of the content in the science textbook matched the North Carolina State Standards? Dennis did not know, but he would find out.

Dennis spent a week in this venture. He began by laying out his standards and benchmarks, assessment measures, and the textbook on his living room floor. When he compared his textbook with the curriculum and test, he could not believe what he discovered. Only 5 chapters out of 18 in his science text contained information that was congruent to what he was supposed to be teaching and what he was testing. This discovery caused Dennis to make some dramatic adjustments in content in his new course outline. Since his science textbook had only 5 usable chapters, he had to put it on the shelf for most of the time. His yearly course outline had to be adjusted to reflect learning goals and objectives that aligned to existing state standards and benchmarks. Dennis began the time-consuming chore of developing aligned units of study to take the place of book chapters, developing assessments, and gathering resources to support the new units.

Dennis was determined to teach what he was supposed to be teaching and what he was assessing. At the same time, he continued to motivate his students and deliver excellent instruction. Before we knew it, it was spring and time for the big test. When the scores came back a few weeks later, our sixth graders were now averaging at the 85th percentile. This increase occurred simply by working on alignment of content.

Can you imagine this happening in your school? Most teachers tell me they can. Under the direction of an outstanding teacher, students tend to learn those things they are taught. The winning combination for student achievement is an outstanding teacher teaching the right things to students.

The following chapter presents a broad conceptual framework that will give you a deep understanding of Total Instructional Alignment. You will find that the TIA process is far more complex than simply teaching those things we will be testing; but it will result in improved student achievement on assessments, so it is well worth the hard work.

Answers to the Dog Test

1. There are four patterns from which to choose:

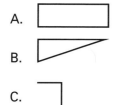

   A.

   B.

   C.

   D.

2. Obedience has to do with how dogs act, whether they obey or follow commands; conformation has to do with how they look or their physical characteristics.

3. All three colors: black, yellow, and chocolate.

4. False.

5. Puppy, Open, Bred by Exhibitor, and American Bred.

6. They are big dogs, and they need a lot of room to exercise and play.

7. Two points must be from major shows.

8. The dog has already received championship status.

9. The dog is judged to be the best representative of its breed at the dog show. After the Best of Breed judging, the dog continues on to compete against other breeds for Best in Show.

10. Characteristics include keen senses, obedience, intelligence, endurance, and stamina.

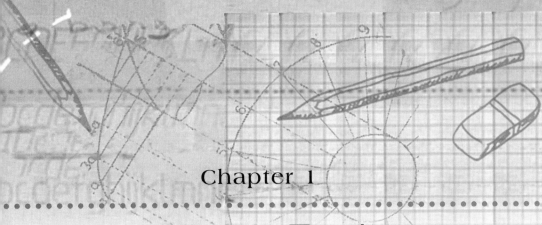

Chapter 1

What Is Total Instructional Alignment?

Have you ever overheard two doctors discussing a medical issue? They use terms with which we are totally unfamiliar, but they seem to understand one another clearly and are able to communicate their thoughts very freely. Most professions have this type of common language that allows practitioners to communicate with one another about the concepts in their field. Educators, however, have developed only a very limited ability to do this. For whatever reason, educators do not seem to have this kind of precise professional vocabulary when it comes to instruction. Half a dozen terms may be used to refer to a single idea, or one common "buzz phrase" can be applied to a number of concepts that are barely related.

"Alignment" is one such word that has entered the jargon of education without any widespread agreement as to its precise meaning. In training sessions, I will often ask principals and teachers to work in small groups to develop a common definition of the term "instructional alignment." Although they all claim to be familiar with the term, they often struggle within their groups to come to consensus on its definition. And I have yet to see two groups yield definitions that are the same. Their definitions often include parts of the alignment process, but it is clear that there is no common understanding of what alignment is and how it works.

There is a lot of power to be gained in developing a common language about instruction. Such a language would allow educators to communicate clearly with one another and would help us develop a shared understanding of important instructional issues. As we prepare to discuss Total Instructional Alignment as a crucial educational process for student success and achievement, it is important to begin by establishing a common understanding of what instructional alignment means and what it looks like in schools and classrooms.

Alignment Versus Teaching the Test

Before defining what Total Instructional Alignment is, it is necessary to discuss what it is not: *teaching the test*. When teachers hear the words "instructional alignment," they frequently believe that they are being asked to teach the test to their students in order to increase test scores. Teaching the test is knowing what questions will appear on the test and teaching the answers to students in an attempt to help them improve their scores. Unfortunately, we sometimes hear stories of this occurring in our schools. The pressure that accompanies high-stakes testing is great for both teachers and students, but teaching the test is not only very unfair to students, it is dishonest and could very well cost educators who try it their teaching licenses.

In fact, most high-stakes standardized tests today cannot be "taught"—and attempting to do so can lead to disaster. Many years ago, when I was teaching first grade, our district decided to use the California Achievement Test to assess student achievement. It was the first time our first-grade students had ever taken a standardized test. As you might imagine, it was quite an interesting experience. Six-year-olds have little concept of time, so when I told them they had 50 minutes to complete the test, they stared at me blankly. I spent the next few minutes explaining to them why they could not keep the two new sharpened pencils they had been given to take the test. Once the test finally got under way, I had to read the questions to the students, since they were unable to read them.

I vividly remember the first question: "Look at the pictures below. Find the paper clip. Color in the circle under the paper clip." My heart sank as I walked around the room. I could not recall one lesson all year long specifically designed to teach my students to recognize a paper clip. Needless to say, there were some students coloring in circles under objects that were not paper clips.

The following year, there was not a student in my class, or any other first-grade class in the school district, who did not recognize a paper clip when he or she saw one. In fact, most of them learned about paper clips the first day of school. I actually saw a first-grade teacher coming to school one day wearing paper clip earrings. When test time came in the spring of that year, I knew my students were ready, and I was excited. On test day, I had my students open their booklets to page one. I remember reading the first question, and having that very same sinking feeling overcome me: "Look at the pictures below. Find the stapler. Color in the circle under the stapler." My students were all frantically looking for paper clips. I was so frustrated!

So why did they change the test? Actually, they had not changed the test at all. They merely changed the question that appeared on the test. We know test questions will change from year to year. The tested *concepts,* however, will remain the same. After the test the second year, we looked up the tested concepts for the California Achievement Test. Nowhere in the entire test guide did it state that first-grade students should be able to recognize a paper clip. The concept the question referred to was that first-grade students should be able to recognize common classroom objects. By teaching the paper clip in isolation, not only were we cheating in the truest sense of the word, we were cheating our students out of learning the concept they needed to know. If we had taught to the tested concept, we would have continually exposed our students to as many common classroom objects as possible throughout the school year. Then, no matter what object appeared on the test, they would be able to take their knowledge of the concept and apply it to answer the question. We know that test questions will change from year to year, as well they should; however, the tested concepts remain constant (for the most part). One year they may test the paper clip, the next year the stapler, and the following year, the yardstick. If we teach to the tested concept, our students should be successful in answering the questions.

Teaching to the tested concepts is a teacher's moral and ethical obligation. Why is this so? Simply stated, it is not fair to test students on information they have not been taught. Besides, most criterion-referenced assessments are designed specifically to measure student achievement as it relates to established standards and benchmarks. If we are not teaching to the tested concepts, it stands to reason we probably are not teaching the standards and benchmarks we are required to teach either.

Total Instructional Alignment is by no means teaching the test. So if Total Instructional Alignment is not simply teaching the test, then what is it? Total Instructional Alignment means making sure that what we teach, how we teach, and what we assess are congruent.

It makes sense that what we teach is congruent with what we assess. It is equally crucial, however, that our instructional processes—how we teach—are also congruent. This is the point at which many attempts at alignment fail: The most finely tuned curriculum cannot improve student performance if there is no congruent change in the classroom learning environment. Even if we have a crystal clear understanding of the knowledge, concepts, and skills we are supposed to be teaching, and our curriculum is tightly aligned with our assessments, we have not achieved Total Instructional Alignment if our instructional practice in the classroom is to go page by page through a textbook that is loosely aligned with the curriculum.

It helps to think of the Total Instructional Alignment process in terms of three broad and interconnected steps. These steps will help you develop a conceptual framework for the entire process:

1. Alignment of the system

2. Alignment of standards, curriculum, and assessments

3. Alignment of instructional practices in the classroom

Alignment of the System

The first aspect of Total Instructional Alignment is alignment of the system, or systemic alignment. Despite its importance, this aspect of the process typically receives the least attention. Perhaps this is because some systemic issues are extremely complex, and many have been entrenched in education for 100 years. W. Edwards Deming, a pioneer in systems thinking research, suggests that the majority of the problems we encounter in our work does not rest with the people who are trying to do the work, but instead with the system in which those people work (Deming, 1982). This is very true in education. Yet the necessary curriculum and classroom changes discussed here simply cannot occur unless the larger educational system also changes to accommodate them.

My own understanding of the systemic aspect of alignment resulted when I transitioned from my position as an elementary school teacher to a position as a junior-high administrator. I learned a lot from making this transition. One of my most eye-opening experiences came from listening to the conversations of the junior high teachers. Although they were very polite about it, much of the discussion I heard at staff meetings, or even in casual conversation, centered on another group of teachers: the elementary school teachers. As you might guess, they were talking about how poorly the elementary teachers had prepared students for their junior-high experience. The central message of these conversations was that the junior-high faculty was doing the best it could with what the elementary schools sent.

After listening to this kind of talk almost daily, finally, out of sheer frustration, I asked why they were spending so much time talking *about* the elementary school teachers instead of having these conversations *with* the elementary school teachers. One teacher said something I have never forgotten: "Everyone knows the system is set up for teachers to talk about each other, not with each other!" This was true. We never met to talk about these important things. We were physically isolated in separate buildings and had disconnected discussions. And there was another group of teachers just down the road—the high school teachers—who were having the very same disparaging conversations about us! And perhaps even further down the road, at some college or university, there was a group of professors decrying how poorly prepared high-school students are for higher education. I have since come to refer to this phenomenon as "passing the competency buck."

This competency buck–passing syndrome is characterized by the belief that the responsibility for the academic problems of our students rests one level below us. The fourth-grade teacher complains, "I would have taught them to divide, but I spent all year on multiplication. That is a third-grade skill." The third-grade teacher certainly would have taught them their multiplication tables, but she spent all year on double-digit addition with regrouping, a second-grade skill. Of course, the second-grade teacher would have taught double-digit addition with regrouping, but he was too busy teaching the single-digit addition skills students should have learned in first grade. And the first-grade teacher would gladly have taught single-digit addition, but unfortunately, she had to spend the majority of the year on rote counting, number recognition, and the importance of staying in one's seat and not eating the crayons! These were all things students were supposed to have learned in kindergarten. So, is it possible that the kindergarten teacher is responsible for the academic problems our high school teachers eventually encounter? Absolutely not! If you ask them, most kindergarten teachers would smile and reply that they did the very best they could do, given what mom or dad brought in the door on the first day of school.

So where does the responsibility lie? We know that we cannot control what mom and dad bring to school. We recognize and accept that we must work with all of our students, regardless of where they are academically, socially, and emotionally. However, we can do a better job of designing a system for student success, and the first step is to acknowledge that we can no longer see ourselves as a system of independent contractors. It is important for each of us to recognize that as students travel through our educational system, the success they experience will be a result of the collective efforts of everyone in the school system.

To illustrate this point, I often ask teachers to visualize a ladder, the top rung of which represents what we want our students to ultimately know and be able to do when they complete their schooling. At each grade level and subject area, each individual teacher must place a rung on that ladder that represents what students are to learn. As students climb from grade to grade, each rung becomes more complex. If anyone at any grade level fails to place his or her rung securely, there is a gap in the ladder that will slow, or even stop, that student's assent. Since all of the educators along the way must be successful in order for the student to climb the ladder, it makes sense that they should work as a team. Yet too often, each teacher works in isolation, and the resulting failure is blamed on the teacher who was on duty when the student fell off the ladder— even if the real problem may have occurred many rungs below.

We can observe this phenomenon in the way we talk about high-stakes tests. We refer to the assessment we give eighth graders as "the eighth-grade test." Yet this test is actually an assessment of knowledge accumulated between kindergarten and eighth grade—it just happens to be administered by the eighth-grade teachers. If we called it an "accumulated knowledge test," or an "elementary education test," we might think differently about it. Learning is an incremental process, and it takes all of us working together to construct a strong, steady, well-connected learning ladder for students to climb.

There is another, perhaps even more challenging dimension to systemic alignment: designing a system flexible enough to align itself to the learning needs of individual students. Currently, most students have to align themselves to the system in place. The concept of aligning the system to the student, rather than the other way around, has tremendous implications for such things as policy, leadership, and the allocation of resources in our schools.

We know that many of the policies and practices governing our schools are a direct result of embedded ideas and established traditions that stem from an antiquated educational system. For example, our current practices of grouping and grading students may have to be reexamined if we are truly to align the system to the learning needs of all students. If each student is to have the opportunity to learn at his or her own speed, flexible scheduling must be implemented and other time issues will have to be addressed. In turn, these kinds of changes will have tremendous effect on the way we allocate and utilize resources in our schools.

So, can you really change a 100-year-old system—that was never designed to teach all students—into one that aligns to each student's individual learning needs? Success in this effort requires strong and courageous educational leaders at the district and building level, leaders who understand the Total Instructional Alignment process and are willing to do whatever it takes to make it happen. These changes will only happen school by school, courageous principal by courageous principal, with courageous teachers who are up to the task. The district must support the efforts of individual schools. Schools are the largest unit of meaningful change, and school improvement occurs school by school (Lezotte, 1997). The systemic issues will at times present tremendous challenges, but strong leaders understand that each challenge brings tremendous opportunity with it.

Alignment of Standards, Curriculum, and Assessments

The second step of the Total Instructional Alignment process is alignment of standards, curriculum, and assessments. This seems to be what most educators think of first when they hear the term "instructional alignment." This step usually addresses the content teachers teach—the curriculum—and what is assessed. Teachers typically follow curriculum guides to help them make decisions about what students are to learn. If the resources are available, these curriculum guides are often developed at the district level to promote a common understanding of the content across grade levels and subject areas.

Two questions must be addressed immediately: Is the curriculum teachers use aligned to existing standards? And do teachers have a very clear understanding of exactly what students are supposed to learn and how it will be assessed? Often, teachers use the curriculum guide to develop their own annual curriculum maps, as well as quarterly, weekly, and daily lesson plans. This sounds simple enough, but often teachers find that the established learning standards are vague, too broad, open to interpretation, and repeated from one grade level to the next. While curriculum guides sometimes can give teachers more clarity as to what students are expected to learn, the way one teacher interprets a standard or benchmark is often completely different from the way the teacher next door sees it.

A group of teachers I was training once began to discuss the reading process and their curriculum. Three different teachers at three consecutive grade levels indicated that their curriculum guide stated they were to teach "main idea" in reading. I asked, "Exactly what do you teach about 'main idea' at your grade level?" As each teacher began to describe his or her lessons, we were surprised to find that the students in this particular school were being taught the same thing in each grade. It might have been a different teacher and a different method, but essentially the same skill was taught at the same level for 3 years in a row. While this phenomenon is also a systemic issue (as most alignment problems are), it points primarily to a deficit in the alignment of standards, curriculum, and assessment. If we are sure that our curriculum is aligned to existing standards, then we must also be sure that teachers clearly understand what students are supposed to learn and be able to do.

Once we determine that the curriculum is aligned with the standards, we must next ensure that assessments are aligned with the curriculum. Are we assessing those things we are teaching students? The dog lesson from the introduction illustrates that if we are going to hold students accountable for learning, we must first give them the opportunity to learn through our instruction.

Alignment of Instructional Practices in the Classroom

The third step of Total Instructional Alignment is alignment of instructional practices in the classroom. In other words, what happens when the teacher goes into the classroom and closes the door? Although sometimes we are hesitant to admit it, we know the reality is that most teachers can teach students virtually anything they want to teach them. For the most part, students trust the teacher's selection of content. They do not question whether what they are being taught relates to a certain standard or benchmark, or whether it will appear on an assessment at the end of the year. Even principals who are strong instructional leaders readily admit that no matter how closely they monitor lesson plans and how regularly they visit classrooms, it is literally impossible to be in every classroom every day to ensure that the content teachers are presenting is aligned to standards and the curriculum. Ultimately, alignment of instructional practices will depend on the expertise and conscience of each classroom teacher.

Alignment of instructional practices in the classroom requires that teachers understand and deliver instruction in a manner that includes standards, curriculum, and assessment in their daily lessons. To do this well, teachers need the basic tools and processes to teach in a standards-based program. They need to be able to develop clear learning goals in the form of good solid behavioral objectives. These objectives have to be specific and measurable. Many teachers tell me that the last time they had to write their own behavioral objectives was in their college or university preparation program. They stopped doing this themselves after they began teaching because the program or textbooks they were given stated the objectives for them. Since the textbook can no longer be the center of instructional practice, teachers must now develop these learning goals for themselves.

Teachers also must be able to break down broad goals and objectives into the essential learning necessary for students to achieve the goals (a process known as "task analysis" [Hunter, 1989]). These essential learning goals then have to be translated into clear curriculum maps to follow throughout the year. Teachers must also develop classroom assessments that truly measure what they want their students to achieve. It is important to understand the multiple ways to assess what students are learning and how to select and design good classroom assessments. Then there is the arduous task of designing excellent lessons that help students master the defined knowledge concepts and skills. And we cannot forget securing appropriate instructional materials and resources. The list goes on and on. Alignment of instructional practices in the classroom may be simple to discuss, but it is complex to accomplish.

Ensuring that Total Instructional Alignment takes place in every classroom requires skilled teachers working with astute administrators who are true instructional leaders. The ultimate success of Total Instructional Alignment will depend on the support and leadership structures that allow for the monitoring and adjusting of the process as it occurs.

A Conceptual Model

Two simple diagrams help show how Total Instructional Alignment works. The overlapping circles in Figure 1.1 represent an instructional program that has not been aligned. In fact, it represents the typical situation in a school or district that has not made a conscious effort to align its instructional program: well-intentioned teachers, working hard at delivering a very loosely aligned instructional program.

The **instruction** circle represents the overall content—the information, concepts, and skills—that the teacher is actually teaching in his or her classroom (the taught curriculum). The **curriculum** circle represents what teachers are told they must teach

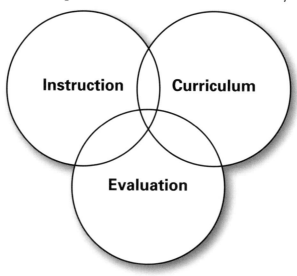

Figure 1.1: A Misaligned Program

(the intended curriculum), and the **evaluation** circle represents the information, concepts, and skills students will be held accountable for through assessment.

Notice that there is only partial overlap between the instruction circle and the curriculum circle; some things in the curriculum are obviously not being taught. Perhaps the teacher planned to teach a science lesson on mammals, but after an incident between students in the hallway just before class, the lesson objective was quickly changed to manners. Manners are not found in the curriculum guide, and while some may argue that they should be, manners are not going to be assessed at the end of the year. We know teachers are still going to teach them in class, however—as well they should. Teachers should be allowed to go above and beyond the parameters of the formal curriculum. They should be given the flexibility to reach beyond the standards and benchmarks to teach more than what is in the curriculum guide. It is important that teachers be allowed to present those things that they think students need to know and to teach those things that excite them as teachers. We know that what excites the teacher is often the very thing that sparks the interest of students and creates an educational experience that students remember long after they leave that teacher's classroom. You can always teach more than what is in the curriculum. It is important to remember, however, that you cannot go above and beyond *at the expense of* what is in the curriculum.

In Figure 1.1, the evaluation circle partially overlaps both instruction and curriculum. This indicates that some things that are assessed are not in the curriculum and did not make their way into instruction. We recognize that well-constructed criterion-referenced test questions measure what is in the curriculum, especially if the curriculum and the assessment both have been designed to reflect the same set of standards. In many instances, however, the high-stakes norm-referenced assessments students are required to take may not be aligned to the standards that direct what teachers are teaching.

The Stanford Achievement Test (SAT) is a common example of a high-stakes norm-referenced test that is not aligned to any specific curriculum. Our conceptual model suggests that if we teach well and students learn what they are taught, then they are sure to get the right answers for those questions that fall where instruction and evaluation intersect. But what if an objective does not make its way into instruction? What if it was never taught to the student—even if it is in the curriculum? Is it possible for students to get the answer to this question right? Well, certainly they could, but there are only two reasons why this could happen. First, the answer may have been part of the student's prior knowledge. The teacher did not have to teach it because the student received the knowledge from another source—a discussion at the dinner table, a show on television, or perhaps from an older brother or sister. Second, if prior knowledge is not the reason the student got the answer right, then the only other explanation is that he or she got lucky and guessed the answer correctly.

There are two groups of students in our schools today: those who can learn without us and those who cannot. Some students learn from us and we know they gain from their experiences with us, but if we were not there, they would still learn. Someone at home would make sure it happens. These students do not depend on school as their sole source of academic learning.

The other group of students we serve—those who cannot learn without us—is a population that seems to be growing. These students do not necessarily have the advantages in their homes that provide the opportunities to learn the kinds of things we assess in school. These students depend on us as their main source for academic information. If we were not there, academic learning simply would not happen for them.

It is important that we not mistake a lack of student access to prior knowledge—a lack of *opportunity* to learn information—for an *inability* to learn information. Advantaged and disadvantaged students both can learn and learn very well. However, we know that they will only learn those things that they are taught.

For years, schools have used scores from standardized tests that were not properly aligned to instructional programs and practices to determine if students would be placed in compensatory programs. It is hardly surprising, then, that these compensatory programs are usually full of a disproportionate number of poor and disadvantaged students. How many of these students have been labeled as having special learning needs not because they could not learn the information on the assessment, but because they never had the opportunity to learn because the information was never taught?

Compare Figure 1.1 with Figure 1.2, which represents a program that has been aligned using Total Instructional Alignment.

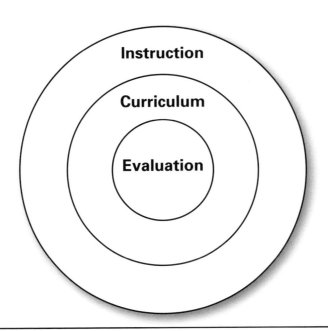

Figure 1.2: An Aligned Instructional Program

Observe both the size of the circles, which represents the amount of content, and the order in which they appear. Notice that the instruction circle is the largest circle and it encompasses both curriculum and evaluation. It stands to reason that teachers are going to teach more than what is contained in the curriculum guide. However, it is important to note that the curriculum circle is contained within the instruction circle. In other words, while instruction may go beyond the curriculum, no part of the curriculum is excluded from instruction. Finally, the evaluation circle is contained inside the curriculum circle. It is the smallest of all the circles because assessments typically do not assess everything in the curriculum. Most assessments are designed to "spot check" to determine whether students have learned what is in the curriculum. Also note that if the assessment or evaluation objective does not measure what it is in the curriculum, it still falls within the circle of instruction. This is important if we are concerned about giving *all* students the opportunity to learn the information that is being assessed.

We know that drawing circles is easy; being able to ensure that aligned instruction is happening in every classroom is much more complex. So, how do we move from a loosely aligned instructional program to ensuring that all students are receiving a program in every classroom that is totally aligned? To make this happen, teachers need to be prepared to teach in a standards-based program. The following chapters will address the tools and processes teachers need to base instruction on learning standards.

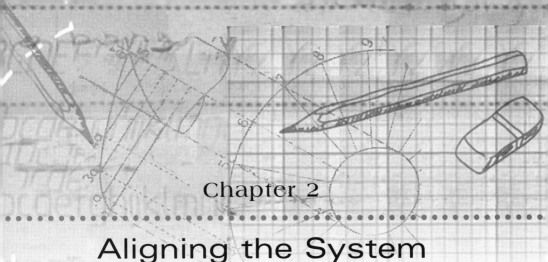

Chapter 2

Aligning the System

Most educators first learned about the birth of our nation's system of public schools in their Foundations in American Education 101 class in college. Among other things, we learned that Horace Mann was credited with founding the first public schools in America. These schools were created on the fundamental belief that everyone was entitled to a free and appropriate education. The idea of educating everyone was an awesome task.

When the first public schools were created in this country, roughly half of the population made a living through agriculture (Economic Research Service, 2000). Children were often expected to work alongside adults on the family farm. Therefore, the school system would have to be designed to cause as little interference as possible with the farming schedule. The schedule that seemed to cause the least disruption to this way of life had students beginning the school year in the fall, after the final harvest. School would remain in session until early spring, when the children would again be needed on the farm for the planting season. Thus, the school calendar included 8 or 9 months of schooling with 3 or 4 months off during the summer.

The traditional school system was based on the factory model. It assigned students to a grade level based on their chronological age. A bell would ring to signal the beginning of the day for students. Each student would have the opportunity to learn under the direction of a teacher or instructor for a fixed amount of time each day. Each grade level would have certain knowledge and skills that students were expected to master before moving on to the next level. At the end of each designated period of time, the bell would signal the group to move to another location, until the final bell let teachers and students know when it was time to go home. This system held time as a constant. In other words, everyone was given the same amount of time to learn the same amount of content in each course or at each grade level. If they were successful, students would be "promoted" to the next grade level. If they were not successful, they would be retained at the same level to try again the next year. Those students who experienced academic failure could choose to leave the school system and return home to continue their work on the family farm.

Obviously, our lives have changed dramatically in the past 100 years. However, the traditional system of educating students has virtually remained the same. In this new era of standards-based and assessment-driven instruction, almost every aspect of the traditional educational system will have to be closely reexamined to determine whether or not it will promote or hinder us in accomplishing the new mission of schools: education for all. Total Instructional Alignment, then, is not simply a classroom requirement or even a school requirement. It is a holistic process that will involve redesigning, redefining, and aligning the entire educational system to meet the individual learning needs of each and every student.

The first step is to acknowledge that many of our past practices in the traditional educational system are actually the exact opposite of what we know about students and how they learn. I call this "knowing better than we do." For example, here are three things we know about students and how they learn:

1. **Students come to school with differing amounts of knowledge and at different skill levels.** I have yet to hear

a classroom teacher argue with this statement. In fact, teachers often tell me that they believe the divide between the student who knows the least and the student who knows the most is getting even wider. Students do not enter school at the same starting point academically, socially, or emotionally; therefore, their instructional needs will vary.

2. **All students can learn, but they do not necessarily learn at the same rate.** John Carroll, a researcher at the University of North Carolina at Chapel Hill, is credited for giving us much insight into this idea through his research on aptitude. According to Carroll (1963), aptitude is not how much a person could learn, but rather the rate at which a person learns. The way this applies in school is that we no longer refer to students as good learners or poor learners, but rather as fast learners or slower learners, depending on their aptitude in a given subject. Carroll's resulting formula for learning is that the degree of learning equals time spent trying to learn divided by the time needed to learn. Therefore, all students can learn if they are given the time they need, assuming they are motivated to do so.

3. **Learning is, for the most part, an incremental process.** We know that learning is a building process. Each piece of knowledge builds upon the last. For example, if a student can write a word but not a sentence, it would be difficult for the teacher to teach that student to compose a paragraph. The student must first be able to write sentences before combining them into paragraphs. Likewise, if a student cannot multiply, it would make little or no sense to try to teach the student long division, since multiplication is a step in the long-division process. Because learning is an incremental process, we cannot expect students to be successful if they skip necessary increments of the learning process.

Given these three things, it is unreasonable for us to expect all students to be successful in a traditional educational system designed after the factory model. The Total Instructional Alignment process first requires a close examination of the system—specifically, current classroom and team structures and the role of leadership in supporting change at the school and district levels.

Classroom Structures

The factory model of education spawned numerous classroom structures that are not compatible with the goal of learning for all: time as a constant, placement by age, and traditional grading procedures. These must be addressed if we are to truly align the system.

Time Versus Learning as a Constant

If we are to successfully teach all students, time must be viewed as a variable and learning as a constant. Figure 2.1 helps to visualize this idea.

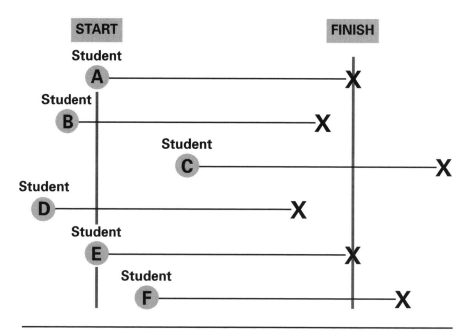

Figure 2.1: The Academic Race

Notice that the students in Figure 2.1 are not lined up at the same place to begin the race. Their varied starting points represent the differences in their knowledge and skill levels. Some students come to us right where we expect them to be academically, while others may be behind, and some may even be ahead. Although we understand that learning is incremental and varies significantly from individual to individual, we give all students basically the same amount of time to learn the same amount of content: 180 days a year, 6 hours a day, 50 minutes per period.

Thus begins the race that starts in September and continues until June. At the end of the race, we evaluate how well our students did. Notice what happened to Student A. This student was able to learn the given amount of content in the given amount of time. This would indicate that Student A is now ready for the next grade level or course. Student B is a different story. This student did not quite make it to the finish line, not necessarily because the student could not have learned the material, but rather because time ran out for that particular student.

How is the traditional educational system designed to deal with Student B? Usually there are two options. The first option is to send that student on to the next grade level or course even though he or she did not master some of the required knowledge and skills. The second option is to send the student back to repeat the whole race again. In our traditional school system, this is known as retention.

Finally, notice that Student C started out ahead of the others and actually went far past the finish line. This student actually learned more than was required. How does the traditional educational system deal with this student? Usually by bringing him or her back to the instructional starting line with the others the next year.

It is obvious that an educational system that holds time as a constant causes learning to become a variable. If we are going to reinvent our educational system to meet the needs of all students, learning must be made the constant; and when we make learning the constant, time will have to become the variable.

Placement by Age

Placing students for instruction based on their chronological age has also become an accepted practice of our traditional educational system. Most students are placed in grades for instruction with other students who are about the same age. This practice raises the question, is what someone knows and is able to do attached in some way to his or her chronological age? Most people would say no. I often use the following example—the piano lesson—to illustrate this point during training sessions.

I began my college education as a piano major before deciding to pursue a career in education. So, if I wanted to, I could teach a class of students to play the piano. Before I begin my lesson, I would want to know how many of my students already know a few piano skills, so I would ask the following questions:

1. **How many people in the group already know how to play the piano?** I inevitably find there are some piano players in the group. Since these people are already doing what I am supposed to teach them to do, it would be my job to increase their existing skill level. Perhaps this would mean introducing them to new composers, working on speed, or improving technique.

2. **How many people cannot play the piano, but do play another musical instrument and know how to read music?** Usually there are some people in the session who fall into this category. These people obviously do not need a lesson on how to read music; instead, they are ready to learn which notes correspond to the keys on a piano keyboard.

3. **How many people do not know how to read music but could play some songs like "Chop Sticks" or "Heart and Soul" by ear?** The people in this group have at least had their hands on a piano at some point in their lives. Since they cannot read music, they are not ready for a lesson on how notes correspond with keys on the keyboard. Their instruction must begin with how to read music.

4. **How many people, when presented with pictures of musical instruments, could pick out the piano?** There are always a few people who fall into this group. These people have absolutely no experience with music or the piano. They definitely must start from the very beginning.

After assessing the knowledge and skills of the group, I find that one lesson will not fit the learning needs of all the participants. Therefore, it is not only logical but necessary to form groups for instruction based on their current *achievement* levels. This should not be confused with the traditional practice of static grouping based on ability, in which students remain in the same group despite their changing skills and knowledge. Achievement grouping is flexible; as students learn, groups are re-formed to address current needs.

Compare this grouping by achievement to the effect of grouping my piano students based on chronological age. What if I decided to form three instructional groups: people aged 45 and older, 35- to 44-year-olds, and those 34 and under? Most people find this illogical. Why, then, do we group students for instruction in our schools based on chronological age? The most honest answer to that question is likely this: because we have always done it that way!

Teachers can accurately determine what students already know in relation to what it is they are expected to learn by using diagnostic information, such as pre-assessments and good questioning strategies. This information can help teachers make sound instructional decisions about what students need to learn. It can also help them determine the most appropriate flexible grouping patterns if there is a need to group students for instruction. It will also ensure students receive the appropriate level of instruction so they are successful in meeting specific learning goals.

Grading Procedures

The academic race in Figure 2.1 also brings into question the grading policies used to evaluate student progress. Student A and Student B actually ran the same race: The two lines on the diagram are identical. Student B tried just as hard as Student A to make it to the finish line, but time simply ran out for Student B. So how would one go about fairly grading the two students? Does the student who finished the race get the highest grade, even though the other student learned just as much? Would it not make more sense to write a description about the learning that occurred during the race? While a re-examination of grading policy threatens more than 100 years of tradition in education, student progress has to be reported meaningfully if we truly want all students to meet or exceed learning standards.

The traditional school system calls for restructuring not only in the way it organizes and deals with students, but also in the way it views teaching. The traditional school system has in the past afforded little opportunity for teachers to communicate, plan, and evaluate the instructional program on a regular basis—especially with the grade levels above and below them.

Team Structures

I remember vividly the first day of my teaching career. I was assigned to teach first grade. All four first-grade classrooms were side by side, making it fairly easy for me to communicate with the other first-grade teachers. While we were given 45 minutes each week for formal planning, we found ourselves planning more often because we were eating lunch or out on the playground together at the same time each day. Virtually everything we did, we did as a grade-level team. This structure helped us to align our programs horizontally. Our planning sessions focused on field trips, lesson plans, themes, pacing, assessments, discipline, programs, resources, methods, and an occasional war story or two. We spoke very little about what was happening in the grade above us or below us— aside from the occasional complaint about what had *not* happened in the kindergarten classrooms.

As a grade-level team, we obviously had content in common. We taught basically the same knowledge, concepts, and skills to students who were about the same age. This is not unlike the way departmental teams function on the secondary-school level. This structure tended to focus our team meetings on the objective of *improving our teaching*. This traditional grade-level—or horizontal—planning is very important for teachers. But what if schools found a way to implement another structure to allow teachers to communicate, plan, and evaluate *vertically?* These vertical team structures would help ensure a logical, sequential progression of knowledge, concepts, and skills from grade to grade or course to course.

Vertical Teams

I saw the power of vertical team structures at a planning session at an elementary school in Ohio. The principal had given the vertical team a 90-minute block of planning time each week to talk about how they were going to use the new structure to meet the learning needs of their students. Never having done vertical planning before, the teachers were initially frustrated by the change. They were not really sure where to begin. Since the team was comprised of kindergarten, first-, second-, and third-grade teachers, I suggested they might want to begin by allowing the third-grade teacher to talk about learning expectations at her level. The third-grade teacher immediately jumped on the opportunity as if she had been waiting a lifetime. She said, "I don't know if this is a learning expectation for others, but I sure wish that the students knew their continents when they got to third grade. My job is to teach countries, but for some reason the students don't know their continents. I can't teach countries until they know their continents, and each year I have to go back and teach the continents myself before I can move on." Then she said to the other teachers on the vertical team, "You guys have had these students for 3 years and there are only seven continents. What seems to be the problem?"

The kindergarten teacher quickly responded, "All my students know all seven continents when they leave my class!" The first- and second-grade teachers did not say anything. Then the kindergarten teacher looked at the third-grade teacher and asked, "When you teach the continents, do you make Africa orange?" The third-grade teacher seemed quite perplexed. Evidently, the kindergarten teacher used an instructional puzzle on which the continents were coded by color. "Africa is orange, Australia is pink, South America is blue," she went on to explain to the others. Still, the first- and second-grade teachers sat in silence.

Then I asked the first- and second-grade teachers what they had taught their students in the past about continents at their respective grade levels. The first-grade teacher said, "We don't teach continents in the first grade." When I asked why, she responded, "Because they learn them in kindergarten!" The second-grade teacher said pretty much the same thing.

So what does this mean for students? They entered kindergarten and learned what the teacher taught them: Africa is orange, Australia is pink, and so on. The students then traveled 2 academic years through the same school, and what they learned in kindergarten never came up again. Now they enter grade three, and the teacher holds up seven squiggly shapes that all look pretty much alike, and asks them to identify Africa. The students are unable to recognize their continents in grade three, and these four teachers are trying to figure out why. Clearly, this was not a student problem.

Nor was it a teacher problem. It was a systemic problem that arose because these teachers had never been given the opportunity to discuss what they were teaching from grade to grade.

These same four teachers were able to correct this curriculum problem within seconds in their new vertical team. The kindergarten teacher said, "I will continue to teach the continents, but I will also continue to color-code them using my instructional puzzle."

The first-grade teacher said, "Fine. When you send them to me, I will assume they know their continents by color and shape, and by the end of the year, my job will be to have them knowing them by shape and word." Then the first-grade teacher asked the kindergarten teacher to send her the color code of the instructional puzzle she uses in her classroom so she could use the same color code.

The second-grade teacher then responded, "So when I receive the students from the first grade, I can assume they know their continents by shape and word. Since a year is a lot of time to forget, my job will not be to teach it, but to simply review it with my students throughout the year."

The third-grade teacher sighed and said, "Thank you!"

How often does this happen to students? The point of confusion was not *what* was taught, but rather *how* it was taught. If these four teachers could solve the continent issue in seconds in their new vertical team structure, what could they do with double-digit addition with regrouping? What about main idea in reading comprehension? Or perhaps fact and opinion and predicting outcomes? This vertical structure enables teachers to begin to sequence a strong, organized, and connected curriculum for students to learn as they move from grade to grade or course to course.

Some schools have taken the vertical team structure even further by assigning groups of students to vertical teams of teachers who they then stay with for 3 or 4 years. In addition to clarifying learning expectations, teachers in these vertical teams have the opportunity to group students by achievement in flexible groups rather than by chronological age.

An elementary school in North Carolina has been doing a wonderful job implementing the idea of vertical teaming for several years. This school serves students in grades two through five. Teachers and students are placed in vertical teams called learning communities. The students remain on the same team throughout the 4 years they are in this school. Teachers in the vertical team plan instruction based on individual student needs. Diagnostic assessments developed for each unit of instruction in reading and math are used to determine students' knowledge of individual skills. Grouping and placement of students is based on what they know and are able to do, and not necessarily on their chronological age. However, students do spend scheduled time each day with their peers of the same age group. Teachers design opportunities for students to interact during instructional and noninstructional time. Teachers plan reading and math instruction to occur at the same time each day so they can use flexible groupings if necessary. Students return to their chronological age groupings for science and social studies.

In this school, instruction is clearly not about sending students on because they are bright or sending students back to get "fixed." The staff uses the strengths of the four teaming teachers to diagnose student needs and prescribe precise instruction, making sure it is at the correct level of difficulty for each individual student. This is not to say that horizontal structures for teaming are not in place as well. Teachers in this school spend time planning both horizontally and vertically. Of course, there are still times when students may not be grouped at all. Whole-class, teacher-directed activities may occur anytime throughout the day. The end goal is that all students meet or exceed the rigorous learning expectations that have been set by their state's standards.

Teachers often tell me that they can visualize how this might work, but they worry that systemic barriers would not allow for vertical teaming. Total Instructional Alignment does require a reexamination of traditional grade-level teacher assignments and student placement policies. For example, teacher certification may not allow vertical teaming opportunities for teachers. The teacher who is only certified to teach kindergarten may not be seen as qualified to work with first graders. This may be a particular issue at the high-school level where teachers are more likely to be certified in specific content areas; however, many high schools are beginning to find creative ways to flexibly group students for instruction based on specific academic needs. I have visited high schools where vertical teams are in place and functioning well. Administrators and teachers in these schools place core classes together toward the middle of the day and elective classes at the beginning and end of the day. This frees up time for vertical teams. Teachers and administrators must ensure that there are no violations of requirements or policies. Sometimes it may be possible to acquire waivers or exceptions to the requirements if it can be determined this is in the best interest of students. Of course, the old systemic barriers of Carnegie units and accumulated seat time still have to be addressed. If we are to fulfill the new mission of leaving no child behind, the old system will have to be redesigned to meet this challenge.

Leadership

Changing a system that has been in place for more than 100 years is not an easy task. Those who seek change will often meet with resistance. Teachers may feel powerless over the system. Clearly, they cannot transform the system by themselves, but they are definitely not powerless! Accomplishing Total Instructional Alignment systemically requires courageous leadership at all levels. Classroom teachers can help put in place the policies, resources, and support structures necessary to accomplish the task if they have the support of strong, instructionally focused principals and support staff at the building and district levels.

Managing Learning Data

Managing the learning data of individual students requires a radical departure from the way things have been done in the past. As an assistant principal in a junior high school, I always had ready access to student attendance data on a daily—and even an hourly—basis. If a student was in first period and did not show up for second period, I knew it within 3 minutes of the class bell; however, I did not have the same well-developed system to track student learning. I have since had the opportunity to work with schools and districts that are beginning to understand how to collect and use data to monitor student learning. Many of these schools are using technology to track student progress and help group students for corrective action or enrichment opportunities.

Both school- and district-level administrators, working in collaboration with teachers, must develop a data-based system to generate, implement, and evaluate instructional decisions. For example, teachers who align their instruction in a standards-based program will need the necessary curriculum materials, resources, and teaching tools to accomplish the task. I often hear teachers exclaim, "If the information is not in my textbook, how will I secure the resources I need to teach?" The implications for school- and district-level budget priorities are great. Principals and district-level administrators must provide the necessary leadership to ensure that money is allocated for the appropriate materials and resources. Teachers must be a part of this decision-making process, since they will ultimately be the ones who will be putting the resources to use in the classroom on a daily basis.

In the Total Instructional Alignment process, improvement must focus on targeted areas of the complete instructional program over an extended period of time. Every year, teachers must be provided with opportunities to reflect and evaluate on the instructional program through a close examination of the student learning data they have collected. This should be done formatively throughout the year to gain the information necessary to adjust instructional opportunities for students and also as a summative evaluation at the end of the school year to reflect on overall instructional effectiveness.

A former superintendent used to draw an analogy for educators in his district by telling a story about the men and women who serve on aircraft carriers at sea. According to this superintendent, at the end of each day, the men and women on the carriers walk shoulder-to-shoulder across the deck searching for and picking up pieces of small debris that might interfere with the takeoff or landing of the aircraft the next day. During this time together, they discuss the day's events. They talk about what went well and what they need to improve. I have worked with schools that spend the last few days of the school year "walking the deck." After students have been dismissed, they examine the data to make their evaluations about student learning and use what they learn from the data to adjust the instructional program for the upcoming school year.

Supporting Professional Development

If we ask teachers to align instruction to the learning needs of individual students, then it only stands to reason that professional development must be aligned to the instructional needs of individual teachers. As teachers are asked to make dramatic changes in the way they teach, professional development and support must be readily available to help them be successful. Major change is often difficult for anyone, but major change without the necessary professional development support and follow-up for teachers can prove disastrous. Perhaps this is why so many reform initiatives of the past have failed. Many often start with a bang, but lack the built-in follow-up and support mechanisms to sustain them, so they fail. As a result, teachers and administrators may look at change with skepticism at best. Providing quality professional development, based on need with designed follow-up and support, is imperative if change is to occur. It is equally important that strategies to sustain the reform are designed into the process as well. This could be in the form of continued professional development to build on previously acquired knowledge and skills, or new staff induction programs that help acclimate new teachers to the school or district.

Providing Administrative Support

Total Instructional Alignment is not a program or an event. It does not take place during a summer workshop. It is an ongoing process and must be developed and improved upon year after year by administrators and teachers. It is imperative that administrators and support specialists at the district level coordinate activities, resources, and programs with school-level educators. District-level personnel must provide leadership and act as a strong base of support for school-level administrators providing leadership in the Total Instructional Alignment process. While change occurs school by school, it cannot occur without district support. Much of the decision-making power that can either promote or impede the process of Total Instructional Alignment rests at the district level.

Principals play a critical role in the Total Instructional Alignment process. As new data emerge, as changes are made to standards, curriculum, and assessments, and as new research evolves around the teaching process, principals must remain on the cutting edge and provide instructional leadership. Without the support of the building-level administrator, it is doubtful if Total Instructional Alignment can be successfully achieved.

Parents must also understand and support the Total Instructional Aligment process. It will be up to school leaders to keep parents involved and informed. Research clearly indicates that effective school programs work hard to establish and maintain strong home, school, and community support of the instructional program (Lezotte, 1991). Some of the systemic changes in the Total Instructional Alignment process may be dramatically different than the traditional way parents have come to view school. Therefore, it is crucial that parents are informed and involved when important decisions are made about the school program.

Perhaps one of the most important roles of leadership in the Total Instructional Alignment process is making sure there is time available for teachers and administrators to work on these important issues. Teachers will need strong support and opportunities to collaborate with each other both vertically and horizontally. The question I am most often asked by teachers during training sessions is, "We know this is important, but where will we find the time to do it?" I believe the Total Instructional Alignment process, coupled with outstanding instruction in the classroom, provides the keys to student success. If this is true, how can we afford not to allocate time for this process? Since time outside the teacher's instructional day may be limited, it is necessary to look at the way we are using our existing time in staff and team meetings and in our opportunities for general planning, professional development, and collaboration. Since we cannot create more time, it will be up to school leaders to find ways to reallocate the time we have towards the purpose of Total Instructional Alignment.

A Changing System

By now it should be apparent that Total Instructional Alignment will not happen overnight. Nor will it happen if it is left to chance. The Total Instructional Alignment process must be thoughtfully designed, implemented, and monitored.

The first step in Total Instructional Alignment is alignment of the system. To do this, we must design an educational system that is flexible enough to align to the learning needs of all students. We must begin by dramatically evaluating every aspect of our existing education system and reexamining many of our practices and policies. As we plan for the future, we may have to rely more on our dreams of what schools can be rather than on our memories of the way things used to be. Questioning a system that embodies more than 100 years of tradition and accepted practice will certainly bring challenges. While the learning process is located in the classroom, it is dependent upon the resources, policies, and demands of the larger school system. Only when those elements are aligned to the needs of students—rather than to administrative expediency or outdated tradition—can teachers be expected to carry the alignment process to the level of individual student instruction.

Now that we have addressed alignment of the system, the next important step in the Total Instructional Alignment process is the alignment of standards, curriculum, and assessment. Often this can be an overwhelming task for teachers. Chapter 3 will address the importance of this step for instructional effectiveness and examine how teachers can ensure clarity about what they are expected to teach and what their students will be expected to learn.

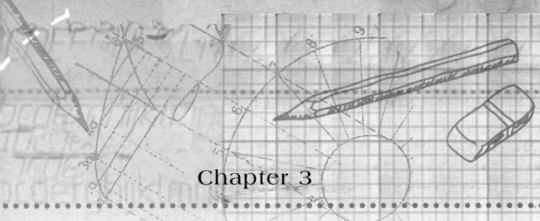

Chapter 3

Aligning Standards, Curriculum, and Assessment

The dog lesson from the introduction is a not-so-subtle reminder of the problems we may encounter when curriculum and assessment are not properly aligned. I really like teaching the dog lesson during my training sessions, and participants seem to enjoy it. They commend me for being prepared, engaging everyone, using visuals, inserting humor into the lesson, teaching to different learning styles, and using effective teaching strategies. This great lesson, however, does not usually bring about great results on the dog test.

What if I added some new teaching innovations to the dog lesson? I could use state-of-the-art technology to teach the lesson, create a brain-compatible environment, use dynamic instructional grouping based on detailed running records—the list goes on and on. But would this impact scores on the dog test? No, because these cutting-edge instructional methods, as important as they are in our classrooms, cannot correct my content errors.

The dog lesson does not yield successful results for one simple reason: I have not aligned what I am teaching and what I am assessing. No matter how well I teach, the best the participants—all college-educated teachers and administrators—typically can do on the dog test is an average score of 50%. New innovations will not increase scores; they can only be effective if I am teaching what I am testing. And this alignment is even more critical than ever before considering the importance of assessment in the lives of today's students.

Formal Assessments

For many years promotion and retention in our schools was linked directly to earned grades and teacher judgment. If students came to school regularly, tried hard, and earned decent grades, they often found themselves being promoted to the next grade. But if their grades were poor, they did not put forth effort, or they did not come to school on a regular basis, they were held back in the same grade for another year.

Now, more than ever before, formal assessments play a critical role in evaluating student achievement in the classroom, and the stakes can be very high for students. Today many states are adopting policies that link promotion and retention directly to results on high-stakes assessments. More often than not, students must now pass some form of assessment in order to receive a high school diploma. Simply attending class and trying hard is no longer enough.

Another way assessments impact students is through the use of tracking. Even though educators are well aware of the impact tracking can have on students, the practice still exists in some form in far too many schools. Often the practice is directly linked to performance on assessments. High school graduation tests are one example. Those students who do not pass the assessment the first time are placed in remedial courses designed simply to help them pass. While students are in these classes, they cannot take other courses that may give them greater opportunities after they graduate. Among other things, the practice of tracking can directly affect a student's post–high school options. It may ultimately impact student self-concept and self-esteem.

Test scores can have an even greater effect on students when assessment results are used to place students in special education. Many compensatory educational programs use test scores to label students for placement in special programs such as those for learning disabilities. Once placed, it is often difficult for students to get out of these programs. This does not mean that all grouping practices are bad. For instance, flexible grouping practices in which students are frequently regrouped based on ongoing assessments of achievement in reading and in math may often be helpful. However, the traditional practice of homogeneous grouping—placing students in perceived ability groups and keeping them there for long periods of time—can have a negative long-term impact on students. This static grouping not only impacts student self-esteem but may also influence teacher expectations. Some of us remember whether we were in the red-bird, blue-bird, or yellow-bird reading group, and we knew that the color of the bird had something to do with how well the teacher thought we were able to read.

It is a well-known fact that teacher expectations directly impact student performance. Do you recall the old joke about the substitute teacher who got phenomenal results from a classroom of underachievers? When questioned by the principal about how she had accomplished such tremendous results with these students, she responded that she knew they would do well when she saw their high IQ scores listed on the student roster. The principal replied in amazement, "Those weren't their IQ scores—those were their locker numbers!" There may be something to that joke. High expectations for success are a characteristic of effective schools documented in the research (Lezotte & McKee, 2002). Teacher expectations can directly impact student self-concept and, ultimately, student performance. Because assessment can have such a wide-reaching impact on students, it is critical that every teacher ensure alignment of instruction and assessment so that all students will have the greatest opportunity to do their very best.

Standards

So how do we make certain that there is alignment between what we teach and what we test? Published state standards alone are not always sufficient guides to curriculum alignment. Standards are often stated in vague or broad terms that can be left up to the individual teacher to translate. One teacher's interpretation of the standard may be very different from the interpretation of the teacher in the room next door. Thus, these two teachers may be teaching very different things in response to the same standard. Even with attempts at further clarification, such as benchmarks or grade-level expectations, it still may be difficult for teachers to interpret exactly what they should be teaching in their classrooms.

Another problem appears when standards are not properly aligned from one grade level to the next. Skills should build both logically and sequentially from grade to grade and from course to course. If standards are vague, broad, or repetitious, the standards document might not provide clear guidance for alignment from one grade or course to the next. Benchmarks or learning objectives may be repeated from grade to grade without distinguishing how they are to change from one level to the next. I once encountered a curriculum document where the concept of main idea in reading comprehension was taught beginning in kindergarten and each year thereafter through grade 12. The guide simply stated that students should be able to determine the main idea of a given passage at each grade level. What is missing in such documents is how the concept of main idea should grow and develop in complexity. Without this guidance, the teacher can only guess how the standard should be handled at any given level.

What is needed is a format that enables teachers to clearly compare the alignment of standards, curriculum, and assessments that helps ensure that assessed skills are presented in a logical sequence for the individual learner. A helpful tool teachers can apply to do this comparison is the congruence matrix.

The Congruence Matrix

Many teachers find that constructing a congruence matrix is a necessary first step to aligning curriculum and assessment objectives. Teachers often find that the objectives that define what they are supposed to teach and what they are supposed to assess are located in several different documents and are not organized in an understandable way. This causes them to miss important connections and not see the total picture. The purpose of the congruence matrix is to organize curriculum and assessment objectives visually in one place for closer examination.

Most congruence matrices are constructed one grade level and one subject area at a time. The congruence matrix in Figure 3.1 is an example. The essential elements displayed on a congruence matrix may vary depending upon the format of the state or local curriculum. Even terminology may vary from state to state because of our lack of common language in education. For example, what is referred to as a "benchmark objective" in one state may be referred to in another state as a "grade-level expectation."

Standard	Benchmark for Grade	Criterion-Referenced Test	Norm-Referenced Test

Figure 3.1: Congruence Matrix

Column 1 on the congruence matrix is usually dedicated to an existing state standard. More often than not, this standard is stated in very broad terminology. It can be so broad, in fact, that sometimes the same standard can be found from kindergarten to grade 12. **Column 2** contains the benchmarks (grade-level expectations) for that standard. These are the objectives that clarify what that standard looks like at that particular grade level. They are usually more specific as to exactly what the student is supposed to learn about that standard at a particular grade level. **Column 3** is for objectives that will be assessed on any criterion-referenced test administered by the district. These may take the form of state end-of-grade or end-of-course exams. Teachers can usually secure these objectives from the data they receive at the end of the year in the form of test results. These reports usually contain information on the skills that were assessed and how students performed on each skill.

If the state or district also administers a norm-referenced assessment, the objectives that will be assessed on this test are placed in **Column 4** on the matrix. For high school, that norm-referenced assessment might be the SAT or ACT examination for college entrance. There might be other things that you find useful to place on the matrix, and you may need to create additional columns to do so. When the matrix is completed, all intended curriculum and assessment objectives for the grade-level subject area will be organized in one place. Figure 3.2 shows a completed congruence matrix for sixth-grade social science.

Notice that the first column addresses one of the broad overarching state standards for social science. Column 2 is more specific: It addresses the grade-level benchmark. Column 3 addresses what will be assessed on a criterion-referenced test that will be administered to students at the end of the school year. Column 4 addresses if and how that skill will be addressed on a norm-referenced assessment that will also be administered to students. When this information appeared in four different documents, it seemed

Standard	Benchmark for Grade	Criterion-Referenced Test	Norm-Referenced Test
4.1: Read charts and graphs in a variety of sources.	4.01: Interpret maps, legends, charts, and pictures.	Interpret maps, legends, charts, and pictures in a variety of sources.	Read and interpret charts and graphs—line, circle, and bar.

Figure 3.2: Congruence Matrix for Sixth-Grade Social Science

very overwhelming. By putting the information side-by-side in the matrix, it becomes easier to decipher.

The congruence matrix enables teachers to boil down curriculum to the essence of what they need to teach and what students need to learn. This information can then be translated into classroom maps for the teacher to follow during instruction. These maps are specific as to what exactly the teacher will teach and how he or she will teach it. If there is an assessment objective that is not also a curriculum objective, it will quickly become apparent on the congruence matrix. Many teachers have indicated that constructing a congruence matrix helps them to see connections within the curriculum and therefore begin to better understand how to organize the learning objectives for more fluid instruction. I am always fascinated to hear the important conversations that begin as teachers discuss the information they organize on the matrix. Often, they become curious and ask to see the matrix of the grade level below and the grade level above their own. This is the beginning of horizontal and vertical alignment.

It is often effective for grade-level teams to work together on the construction of these matrices. Some teachers may prefer to create their matrices on a computer. Others prefer to work in a more low-tech fashion with scissors and paste. Teachers often agree that the tactile, hands-on experience of creating large charts by hand and manipulating and organizing the curriculum and assessment objectives helps them better understand and communicate the alignment process. To design matrices in this hands-on way, make copies of curriculum and assessment objectives for cutting and pasting onto large sheets of poster board.

After constructing a congruence matrix, teachers can begin the process of organizing instructional objectives (derived from the matrix) into units of study. Natural groupings of knowledge, concepts, and skills—known as "strands"—are easily recognizable on the matrix. Typically, teachers will find anywhere from four to eight strands depending on the subject. For example, the subject of language arts might contain strands for reading, writing, literature, listening, viewing, and speaking. These strands usually remain consistent from one grade level to the next. The knowledge, concepts, and skills within these strands develop in complexity as the student progresses from grade to grade.

Backward Mapping of the Curriculum

To ensure a logical, sequential progression of skills as students move from grade to grade, teachers must meet and examine the matrices for vertical alignment—alignment between grade levels. As teachers work together to determine vertical alignment, it is important that they look at what they ultimately expect students to know and be able to do and then work backward to map a curriculum that offers strong support at each grade level. This is called backward mapping of the curriculum: Before you create the map, you have a final destination in mind. The old adage "If you don't know where you are going, any road will take you there" also holds true with curriculum.

I once worked with a group of elementary school teachers who had done a wonderful job with horizontal alignment in each grade level but had not worked on vertical alignment of the curriculum. I noticed in their curriculum guide that the "fact and opinion" skill repeated itself every year from second to fifth grade. Each year the learning goal simply stated that the student should be able to distinguish fact from opinion. I asked the second-grade teachers to tell me exactly what it was they taught their students about fact and opinion. After some group collaboration, they replied, "You are wearing black pants today. That is a fact. It is the coldest day I have ever experienced in this city. That is my opinion." In other words, they taught their students the difference between a fact and an opinion. I then turned to the third-grade teachers. I asked them the same question. Believe it or not, they gave me the very same answer! The very same skill was being taught to students 2 years in a row.

I turned to the fourth grade teachers and asked the question, "What do you teach about fact and opinion?" They replied that they expected students to be able to read a two-page passage, *infer* whether or not the author was stating facts or giving opinions, and if the author was giving opinions, determine if he or she used sound or faulty reasoning. During this brief but powerful conversation, I identified what I now call the "Academic Grand Canyon." When I then asked the fourth-grade teachers why they held such high expectations for their students, they replied, "Because that's how students will be assessed on the end-of-year test." We knew we could not change the test. However, we could adjust the support given to the students at grades two and three to prepare them for grade-four expectations.

In backward mapping, it is important to determine the final destination (what we want our students to know and be able to do) and create clear supporting curricular maps with connections from grade to grade and course to course. This means designing curriculum from high school down to middle school and eventually connecting to elementary school. This can be done by clustering a few grade levels to work on vertical analysis of the strands of the curriculum and then connecting the clusters and adjusting the curriculum accordingly. As the vertical adjustments are made, teachers are able to look for holes, gaps, and overlaps in the curriculum. A superintendent I know has dubbed this process most appropriately as "gap analysis." Figure 3.3 is an example of a backward map in the math strand of algebra created by teachers in the Owensboro, Kentucky, Public Schools.

Algebraic Ideas
Owensboro Public Schools Skills Continuum

Preschool

5B.   Copy a pattern from a model (physical clues, clap-tap).

Kindergarten

5B.   Identify and copy a pattern from a picture or model.
5E.   Identify and extend patterns in shapes, colors, and real life.
5A.   Predict what comes next.
5C.   Continue a given pattern.
5D.   Create your own pattern and explain the rule.

First Grade

7D.   Describe patterns in real life, numerical patterns, movements, and sounds.
3E.   Illustrate the repeated pattern in numbers from 0 to 100.

Second Grade

3E.   Create, reproduce, and extend patterns of numbers, movements, sounds, shapes, and objects.
5G.   Explain input-output machines.

Third Grade

5E.   Find solutions to number sentences with missing values (for example, 7 + ? = 10, ? + 5 > 10).
5F.   Substitute numbers in function machines.

Figure 3.3: Backward Map for Algebraic Ideas. Used with permission from Owensboro Public Schools (Kentucky)

Fourth Grade

10F.   Identify rules for patterns (input, output).

10G.   Graph points on a number line (positive numbers only).

10H.   Compare/contrast number patterns.

10I.   Solve equations using variables.

10J.   Represent and describe relationships through the use of variables, ordered pairs, lists in tables, plots on graphs, and patterns.

8C.   Plot coordinates on a line graph.

10C.   Recognize and create number/geometric patterns.

Fifth Grade

9D.   Graph points on a positive coordinate system (Cartesian Grid).

10A.   Explain functions (input and output) through manipulatives, pictures, tables, and words.

10B.   Find solutions to number sentences with missing values (for example, $7 + ? = 10$, $? + 5 > 10$).

10D.   Generate rules for patterns and ordered pairs.

10E.   Analyze how sequences are alike and different (numbers, pictures, words) and describe.

Sixth Grade

8B.   Describe numerical and geometric patterns using words and pictures.

8C.   Illustrate simple patterns as a basic function (input/output) through tables, graphs, and verbal rules.

8D.   Organize data into tables and plot points on a Cartesian Grid (I quadrant).

8E.   Solve problems using simple formulas (for example, $A = lw$).

8F.   Write and solve equations with one variable using concrete and/or informal methods that model everyday situations.

Seventh Grade

7A.   Explain the meaning of variables.

7D.   Substitute answer to check.

7F.   Solve concrete and pictorial equations.

7G.   Write algebraic expressions.

7H.   Represent tables and rules as functions.

7J.   Describe numerical and geometric patterns using variables.

7K.   Recognize, create, and continue patterns. Generalize the pattern by giving the rule for any term.

Figure 3.3: Backward Map for Algebraic Ideas (continued)

7L. Simplify numeric and algebraic expressions.
7M. Solve problems involving formulas.
7N. Interpret relationships between tables, graphs, verbal rules, and equations.
7O. Demonstrate a variety of methods and representations to create and solve single-variable equations that may be applied to everyday situations.
7P. Explain variable expressions as incomplete thoughts with variables in them (not equal signs) and equations with complete thoughts (signs and balanced sides).

Eighth Grade
6B. Simplify numerical and algebraic expressions.
6C. Solve one-step equations and inequalities.
6F. Demonstrate the relationship between tables, graphs, rules, and equations.
6G. Model equations and inequalities.
6H. Understand about functions (graphs, rules, tables, and notation).
6I. Make tables of solutions.
6J. Graph solutions from a table.
6K. Explain how the change in one variable affects the change in another variable.
6L. Recognize, create, and continue patterns (generalize the pattern by giving the rule for the nth term and defending the generalization).
6M. Graph lines using tables.
6N. Demonstrate a variety of methods and representations to investigate inequalities.
6O. Determine the slope and equation of a line by analyzing the line (for example, $Y = mx + b$, m is rise/run, b is y-intercept).

Algebra I
3A. Translate life problems from mathematical to algebraic expressions.
3C. Demonstrate order of operations for evaluating mathematical expressions.
3D. Apply the properties of arithmetic to algebra.
3E. Translate from the concrete level of thinking to the abstract level.
4A. Identify terms, variables, and coefficients.
4C. Combine like terms.
4D. Express fractional coefficients in lowest terms.

Figure 3.3: Backward Map for Algebraic Ideas (continued)

4E. Apply order of operations.

5A. Use basic operations to isolate variables.

5B. Translate words into algebraic symbols and equations.

5C. Graph linear equations by plotting points.

5G. Solve literal equations for indicated variable.

5D. Calculate the slope-intercept form of a line for graphing.

5E. Construct tables of numeric value of equation and inequality.

5F. Recognize parallel and perpendicular relationships using the slopes.

7A. Solve and graph linear inequalities.

7B. Demonstrate difference between equality and inequality.

7C. Solve inequalities.

7D. Graph a solution to an inequality in a coordinate plane.

7E. Apply the concept that multiplying or dividing by a negative reverses the direction of the inequality.

8A. Solve by graphing, substitution, and linear combination.

8B. Identify the types of solutions.

8C. Interpret results when applied to real-life situations.

10C. Solve systems using matrices.

6A. Utilize rules of exponents for numeric and algebraic expressions.

6B. Identify, add, and subtract types of polynomials and their parts.

6C. Identify and factor a common monomial factor.

6D. Multiply polynomials and divide monomials.

6E. Apply the zero product property and know how to relate to factors of polynomials.

12A. Utilize the skills learned to solve linear equations and inequalities to solve numerically, graphically, or symbolically non-linear equations such as quadratic and exponential equations.

12B. Extend ideas of transformations of linear equations, such as vertical and horizontal shifts, to transformations of non-linear equations.

5H. Define a function.

5I. Demonstrate functional notation and graph functions.

5J. Demonstrate how formulas, tables, graphs, words, and equations of functions relate to each other.

9A. Simplify radicals.

9B. Solve linear equations with radical solutions.

Figure 3.3: Backward Map for Algebraic Ideas (continued)

13B. Write and solve proportion sentences.

13D. Solve problems that have direct or inverse relationships for any variable.

Algebra II

5B. Develop functions from data points (linear functions).

9C. Analyze and interpret statistical graphs such as frequency plots.

11A. Solve systems of equations algebraically and graphically.

3A. Apply the zero product property.

3B. Solve quadratic equations by various methods (factoring, quadratic formula, completing the square, graphing).

3C. Apply quadratic equations to finding zero.

3D. Translate real-life situations to quadratic equations.

3E. Find vertex, minimum, and maximum.

4A. Write an equivalent equation or inequality in simplest form.

4B. Determine ordered pairs in a solution set.

4C. Relate ordered pairs, graph, and equation.

4D. Determine domain and range.

4E. Apply analysis of graph to real-life situations.

5A. Identify the attributes of families of functions.

5B. Develop functions from data points (nonlinear).

5C. Describe elements that change and elements that do not change under transformation.

5D. Represent patterns using functions.

5E. Perform operations on functions (add, subtract, multiply, divide, composition, and inverse).

6A. Illustrate the relationship between exponential and logarithmic functions.

6B. Demonstrate the methods of solving simple exponential and logarithmic functions.

6C. Explain the basic properties of and be able to use logarithms to solve problems.

6D. Utilize technology to represent exponential and logarithmic functions and show die graphs.

6E. Explore and explain transformations of these functions.

11B. Solve systems using matrices with and without a calculator.

Figure 3.3: Backward Map for Algebraic Ideas (continued)

This backward map for algebra addresses the knowledge and skills necessary for students to be successful from preschool through Algebra 2. Notice how the learning expectations are clearly spelled out in behavioral terms at each grade level. Each year the skills grow in complexity and every teacher has some level of responsibility to ensure that students learn what they need to be successful at the next grade level. It is important to note that a student's chronological age does not necessarily indicate where the student is in the process of learning. It is only through assessment that we can accurately determine any one student's mastery of the essential learning.

This backward mapping process is like constructing rungs on a learning ladder for the student to ascend. It is up to each teacher to do his or her part as students work their way through the system. If one teacher fails in this task and there is a breakdown at any grade level, the next teacher may have to go back and fix the rung from the previous year.

At the conclusion of the backward mapping process, the district will have a set of clear, detailed guides to the essential knowledge, concepts, and skills students must master at each grade level and in each subject area. These curriculum maps are aligned to the assessments that will measure learning and are aligned from grade level to grade level. This gives teachers specific information about what exactly they are supposed to be teaching and what students are to be learning. Teachers can look ahead at the next grade level to see where their students are headed or below to see what their students should have mastered the year before.

From Curriculum Alignment to Instructional Alignment

The next step is to align the detailed curriculum maps to the daily process of teaching and learning in the classroom. Even the best curriculum guide is all but useless if it sits on a shelf gathering dust and has no impact on instruction. It is up to each individual teacher to do his or her part to ensure that students are learning what is expected at each grade level—to make sure they are successfully making their way up the ladder.

Aligning instructional practice in the classroom is not always as easy as it sounds. Teaching requires depth of content knowledge, resourcefulness, and creativity in the approach to instruction. Since textbooks are not always aligned to standards, it is no longer an acceptable practice to simply stay "one page ahead" of the students when we teach. If teachers do not align instruction in the classroom, the curriculum and assessment alignment efforts of the district will have little or no impact on student learning.

It is simply not fair to teach students one thing and then assess them on something different. To create a level field, it is critical that we give all students an equal opportunity to learn the knowledge, concepts, and skills for which we hold them accountable. Chapter 4 addresses the complexity of alignment of instructional practices in the classroom and outlines the tools teachers need to be successful.

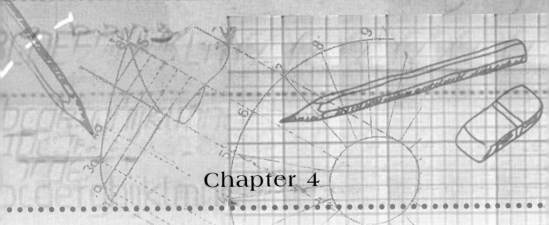

Chapter 4

Aligning Instruction

Many schools and districts have devoted a small fortune in human, material, and financial resources to aligning standards, curriculum, and assessment through the development of aligned curriculum documents. All this work, however, will make little difference if it does not impact instruction at the classroom level. We all know that what happens when the classroom door closes and the teacher begins instruction is what ultimately matters the most.

Before the onset of standards, teachers could teach whatever they thought was important for their students to learn. For example, as a beginning teacher, my favorite social studies unit was one on service jobs (what we called "community helpers," such as police officers, firemen, doctors, and nurses). I developed this unit during a university teaching methods class. I invested many hours in the development of that unit, and I had a wealth of materials to accompany it. I enjoyed teaching it, and the students seemed to enjoy learning about community helpers. In retrospect, I am really not certain that the goals I established in the unit were actually part of the local district curriculum for first-grade students; however, it did not matter at the time. There was no focus on accountability as there is today, no designated testing program designed to measure whether or not students met certain predetermined learning goals.

In most states, this is no longer true. Therefore, it is imperative that teachers make sure students are given the opportunity to learn those things that they are expected to learn and for which they will ultimately be held accountable. Of course there is nothing at all wrong with going above and beyond the basic content when it comes to classroom instruction. Teachers often are able to teach things that they believe are important or interesting to their students—even when the material is not part of the basic curriculum; however, this should not be done *at the expense of* the necessary content.

The Congruence Matrix and Lesson Planning

For alignment of instructional practices in the classroom to exist, teachers must ensure that their lesson plans and other activities are aligned to the intended and assessed curriculum. The congruence matrix presented in chapter 3 is one helpful tool. The purpose of the matrix is to assist teachers in organizing standards, curriculum, and assessment objectives visually in one place. This tool helps teachers focus on the basics of exactly what is to be taught and what students are expected to learn. It also helps teachers see connections within the curriculum and therefore better understand how to begin to organize objectives for instruction for the year. Lesson plans then become the best way to ensure that students learn the essential information. Teachers may choose to teach the information in different ways depending on the needs of the students. Although the "what" students are to learn is the same, the "how"—how the content is translated through lessons in the classroom—may be very different. Most significantly, the matrix helps teachers become more standards- and objective-based in their approach to instruction.

Standards-Driven/Objective-Based Instruction

The alignment of instruction at the classroom level requires teachers to be goal-oriented during both the planning and the execution of lessons. Teachers should begin instruction with clear learning goals in mind and use strategies and activities that are congruent to the established learning goal. All too often, instruction in the classroom is a stringing together of activities. Teachers first decide what activities they want their students to do. After the activity is selected (or sometimes even taught!), the teacher may then go back to the curriculum document to try to match the activity to an objective or goal. I call this approach to instructional delivery "activity-based instruction." In other words, teachers first decide what they want their students to do and only later determine what students should have learned from doing it. Obviously, there are many reasons why this is not the best approach to instruction. For example, teachers may find that there was no learning goal in the curriculum document that matched the activity they selected. Activity-based instruction often results in a "hit or miss" approach to teaching. This can cause a disconnected and fragmented instructional program for the learner in which concepts are dealt with more haphazardly than logically and sequentially.

To truly align instructional practices in the classroom, teachers must first establish *what students are expected to learn* and then determine *the best activity to teach it.* This approach, known as standards-based/objective-based instruction, requires the teacher to begin by establishing clear learning goals and objectives prior to instruction. After the specific learning goal has been established and stated in clear and measurable behavioral terms, the teacher may select those activities and learning experiences that are congruent to and support the intended goal of the lesson.

This may sound easy enough, but the last time many teachers were required to construct a good solid behavioral objective was in college. With textbooks driving instruction for so many years, teachers found that these textbooks and the accompanying teacher's guides already included behavioral objectives with corresponding activities. All the teacher was required to do was execute the lesson suggested in the teacher's guide. Now, unfortunately, the objective or goal stated in the textbook may not be aligned to the curriculum students are supposed to be learning. Therefore, teachers must be prepared to develop their own learning goals and objectives for their daily lessons.

Developing Clear Learning Goals

In order to create clear learning goals, teachers must understand how to construct objectives that can be stated in measurable terms. These are called *behavioral objectives*. Most behavioral objectives reflect the content students are to learn and the level of complexity required in the thinking process necessary to accomplish the objective. More than 40 years ago, Benjamin Bloom conducted extensive research on the levels involved in the thinking process. The hierarchy of thinking identified by Bloom involves six levels of thinking that have become known as Bloom's Taxonomy (1976). The chart in Figure 4.1 gives a quick review of Bloom's Taxonomy.

The first column indicates the cognitive level of thinking, the second column defines the level of thinking, and the third column lists signaling verbs that describe what a student might be doing at that particular level of thinking. For example:

- Knowledge simply means rote memory or recall. If students are listing five characteristics of mammals, they are at the knowledge or memorization level of thinking.

- However, if students are able to describe or explain each characteristic in their own words, then they are demonstrating the comprehension or understanding level of thinking.

- If, when given a stack of pictures of various animals, students are able to classify mammals versus nonmammals based on the five characteristics, they are applying their knowledge.

Level	Definition	Signaling Verbs
Knowledge	Perform rote memory, recall	name, tell, list, say, state, repeat, label, recognize, read
Comprehension	Understand	explain, describe, paraphrase, summarize, show, report, infer, discuss, express, locate
Application	Use in a new situation	use, construct, make, classify, solve, diagram, transfer, dramatize, apply, draw, model
Analysis	Break apart and show relationships between the parts	distinguish, compare, contrast, analyze, examine, combine, take apart, experiment
Synthesis	Put the parts together to create something new	predict, invest, create, design, plan, compose, arrange, hypothesize
Evaluation	Make a valid judgment based on evidence	judge, justify, refute, defend, evaluate, critique, appraise, determine, validate, assess, rate

Figure 4.1: Bloom's Taxonomy

- If students are able to describe likenesses and differences between a given mammal and a nonmammal, then they are at the analysis level of thinking. This means they are able to break the characteristics of both down into their parts and recognize relationships.

- If students are able to design a new mammal possessing the five characteristics that has never walked the earth before, then they are at the synthesis level of thinking. This means they are putting all they know about mammals together to create something new.

- Finally, if students are able to look at the mammals created by other students and judge whether or not they are indeed mammals and give supporting reasons, then they are at the evaluation level of thinking. This means the students are able to make valid judgments based on evidence.

Students today are being assessed on their ability to think at higher levels and not simply on their ability to know and understand information. The questions students are being asked on today's assessments have very little to do with what they can remember or understand. Increasingly, high-stakes test items are designed to assess the student's ability to apply, analyze, synthesize, and evaluate information. Why is this so? Today we have easy and instant access to information. With a simple click of the mouse, we can find out essentially anything we want to know. Therefore, it is important for today's learners to have the ability to access information and then, more importantly, to know what to do with the information once they get it. This means they need to know how to transfer and apply this information into new and different situations. It also means that they know how to analyze the information by breaking it down into its parts so they can see the relationships between those parts. Today's learners must possess the ability to synthesize the information by putting it back together to create something new. Finally, students need to know how to evaluate the information and make valid judgements based on it.

Therefore, teachers must view Bloom's taxonomy as more than just another list. Teachers must be able to take these higher-level thinking skills and actually apply them to instruction on a daily basis. This requires that teachers be able to analyze the goals and objectives in their standards and curriculum. They also need to be able to synthesize and create their own goals and objectives daily for instruction, and finally, they must evaluate these goals and make judgements about whether students are properly engaged in the learning process.

For example, if you ask a student to name or list three characteristics of a mammal and the student responds that mammals have hair, produce milk, and bear live young, this means he or she knows those characteristics. If you then ask what it means to bear live young, and the student replies, "I don't know, but a mammal does it," it probably means that he or she is not at the comprehension level of thinking. In other words, the student can say it, but does not truly understand what he or she is saying. Students are often able to say things they really do not understand, especially if they have good memories. If they do not have the comprehension base, it is practically impossible for them to apply and analyze the information. Learning is an incremental process. You cannot understand what you do not know, and you cannot apply what you do not understand.

Often, the alignment of instructional practices in the classroom is not a content issue. In other words, the teacher is teaching the correct content, but not at the right level of thinking. Students are assessed at higher levels of thinking, but there continues to be a great deal of instruction in the classroom that never goes beyond knowledge and comprehension. It is critical that teachers have a clear understanding of and are able to write behavioral goals and objectives at higher cognitive levels. One way to do this is by using a tool called the Box (Figure 4.2, page 76), which is divided into 4 smaller squares. Each behavioral objective has four basic parts, which fit into the four quarters of the box.

Square 1 is the thinking box. It is the general behavior or level at which you want your students to be thinking. Since this is the

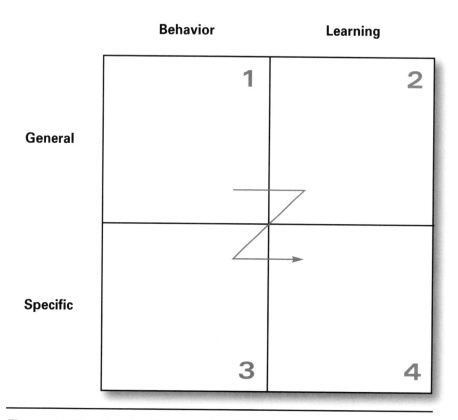

Figure 4.2: The Box for Constructing Behavioral Goals and Objectives

thinking quarter, the only words that will ever appear there will refer to a level of Bloom's Taxonomy: knowledge, comprehension, application, analysis, synthesis, or evaluation.

Square 2 is the general learning box. It is usually the broad area of instruction, such as a strand or unit title. Examples include "Living Things" in general science, "The Cell" in biology, "Fractions" in general math, "Linear Equations" in Algebra, "World Interactions" in social studies, and perhaps "Story Elements" in language arts.

Square 3 is the specific behavior box. It is the doing box because it indicates specific activities that demonstrate that students are thinking at the target level. Since this is the doing box, a verb will always appear in square 3. Squares 1 and 3 must always match. For example, "knowledge" and "listing" match because listing is a knowledge-level activity: It tells you the student has something memorized and is able to recite it as a list.

Square 4 contains the specific content from the broad area or strand at each grade level or in a specific course. The specific content is an outgrowth of the general content. For example, "mammals and their characteristics" is a specific content outgrowth of a broad strand in the area of general science known as "Living Things." In order to turn this into a behavioral objective, you read from square 1 to 2 to 3 to 4 (following a Z pattern) and fill in the words as you go. This objective (Figure 4.3) would then read, "The learner will demonstrate knowledge of living things by listing three characteristics of a mammal." This is a solid behavioral objective that can be measured easily.

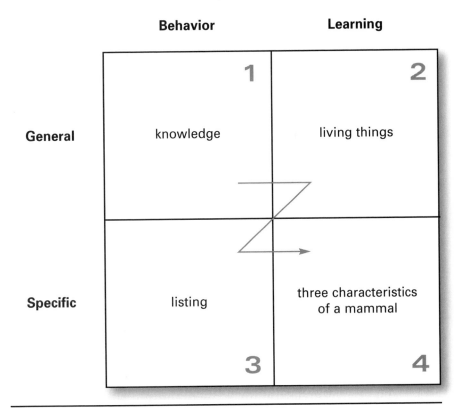

Figure 4.3: Behavioral Objective for Knowledge

To change the level of thinking in this objective to comprehension, simply change square 1 to comprehension. When square 1 changes, so must square 3. The verbs "explain" or "describe" indicate comprehension. Now the objective would read, "The learner will demonstrate comprehension of living things by explaining three characteristics of mammals."

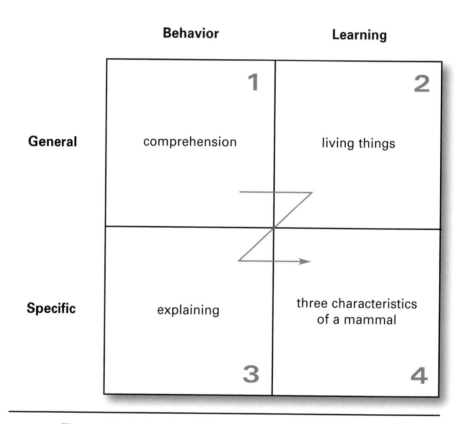

Behavior	**Learning**
1	**2**
General comprehension	living things
Specific explaining	**3** three characteristics of a mammal **4**

Figure 4.4: Behavioral Objective for Comprehension

Again, this could easily be measured by having students explain in writing or to a peer what it means to bear live young, thus demonstrating a higher level of thinking than just being able to list the characteristics. What if you want students to apply their knowledge? The verb you choose for square 3 might be "classify"; your objective would then read, "The learner will apply knowledge of living things by classifying animals as mammals or nonmammals based on three characteristics" (Figure 4.5).

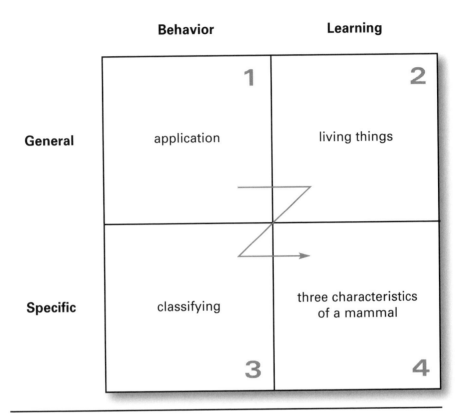

Figure 4.5: Behavioral Objective for Application

This objective can be taken to the synthesis level simply by changing square 3 to the verb "create." The objective changes to, "The learner will synthesize knowledge of living things by creating a mammal possessing these three characteristics that has never lived on Earth" (Figure 4.6, page 80). During the entire process of changing this objective (Figures 4.2 through 4.6) the one thing that remains constant is the content. What does change, however, is the level at which students are thinking and, as a result, what they are doing.

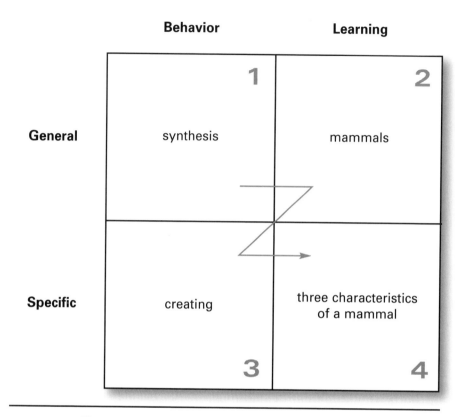

Figure 4.6: Behavioral Objective for Synthesis

Task Analysis

Another important tool for teachers to use when breaking curriculum objectives into concrete lesson plans is task analysis. Madeline Hunter, the noted educator and educational researcher, defined task analysis as the act of breaking a broad learning goal down into the essential learning steps necessary for achieving the goal and then sequencing these steps from the most simple to the most complex (Hunter, 1989). For the most part, task analysis is a very natural process. In fact, we are constantly task analyzing in our daily lives. For example, if our objective is to buy groceries for dinner, we naturally begin breaking down the steps necessary to accomplish the task. We may ask ourselves questions such as:

- Have I decided what I will be serving?

- Have I made a list of the groceries I will need?

- Have I decided at which store I will be shopping?

- Do I know what time I need to leave for the store?

- Do I know when I need to return home?

- Have I decided how I will get to the store?

- How will I pay for the groceries?

All these steps are necessary to accomplish the broader goal of securing groceries for dinner. The task must also be accomplished in a given order. If I have not determined what I will have for dinner, it would be difficult to make a list of the groceries I will need to prepare it. If there are some special foods on my list, it may affect where I will shop. In much the same way, teachers must task analyze learning goals to determine the essential learning necessary to accomplish the goal, and then determine the correct order for instruction. According to Hunter, there are four essential steps to the task analysis process:

1. Determine the learning goal.

For most teachers, learning goals have been predetermined through existing standards, benchmarks, and district curriculum guides. However, these goals and objectives are often too broad for any specific lesson and must be broken down and made more specific. It is important for the teacher to begin with a clear learning goal, and not simply an activity that may or may not be aligned with a standard.

2. Make sure there is a clear understanding of the learning goal.

Teachers are usually given curriculum documents to use in planning for instruction—documents with learning goals and objectives established by a state or district committee. Sometimes the language can be broad or vague and may rely on unfamiliar terminology. Since most states have already formulated state standards as learning objectives, teachers need to be sure they understand what that standard means before beginning to break it down. It is important for teachers to be clear about the learning goal and how they will assess the goal to determine student mastery.

3. Identify the learning steps necessary to accomplish the goal.

Once the teacher has established a clear understanding of the broad learning goal, the next step in the task-analysis process is to break the goal down into the essential learning necessary to accomplish the goal. This usually takes the form of a brainstorming process centered on the question, "What would a student have to know and be able to do in order to accomplish this goal?" At this stage, it is more important to focus on the necessary learning and not worry about the order of instruction. For example, in order to tell time to the hour on an analog clock, students must first be able to recognize numbers 1 to 12, understand the difference between the long hand and the short hand, and so on.

4. Establish a logical order for instruction.

After the essential learning has been identified, the final step in the task analysis process is to establish the correct order for instruction. Sequencing the learning from the most simple to the most complex usually accomplishes this.

Figure 4.7 shows a task analysis of a noncognitive objective, freestyle swimming, broken down into the essential learning steps and sequenced from the simplest to the most complex step.

Notice that this objective is broken down from the most basic beginning step of getting into the water. When teachers task analyze cognitive objectives, they need to determine the essential things students must know and be able to do to accomplish the objective. This further clarifies what must be taught and what students must learn. Figure 4.8 (page 84) shows an example of a cognitive task analysis.

Unit Objective: Upon completion of this unit, the learner will swim freestyle across the pool for a distance of 50 yards.

Task Analysis: Can the learner . . .

1. Get in the water?

2. Hold his or her breath?

3. Put his or her face in the water?

4. Kick with the assistance of a kickboard?

5. Demonstrate proper arm strokes and breathing techniques?

6. Coordinate arm strokes and kicking action?

7. Coordinate arm strokes, breathing techniques, and kicking action?

8. Coordinate proper freestyle techniques to propel a distance of 10 yards without assistance?

9. Coordinate proper freestyle techniques to propel a distance of 20 yards without assistance?

10. Swim freestyle across the pool a distance of 30 yards without assistance?

11. Swim freestyle across the pool a distance of 40 yards without assistance?

12. Swim freestyle across the pool a distance of 50 yards without assistance?

Figure 4.7: Task Analysis of Freestyle Swimming

Learning Goal: The student will demonstrate his or her ability to evaluate the author's opinion by justifying the author's opinion from facts found in a story.

Task Analysis: The learner can . . .

1. Define the terms "fact" and "opinion."

2. Give an example of a fact and an opinion.

3. Classify statements as facts or opinions.

4. Formulate examples of statements containing facts and opinions.

5. Determine faulty reasoning of an author's opinion.

6. Justify whether a statement is a fact or an opinion (using the author's purpose).

7. Locate facts and opinions in a variety of sources (advertisements, propaganda, and so on).

8. Explain the author's viewpoint.

9. Evaluate reliability of the source.

10. Assimilate knowledge and strategies of fact and opinion into various forms of writing.

11. Formulate an opinion based on information presented in a passage.

12. Evaluate the author's opinion by justifying his or her opinions from facts found in the story.

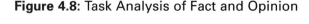

Figure 4.8: Task Analysis of Fact and Opinion

Because student knowledge and skills vary in most classrooms, students can be at many different places on the task-analysis scale at any given time. Therefore, in order to meet individual learning needs, teachers must become diagnostic and prescriptive when it comes to instruction. They must accurately identify the learning needs of individual students, and then prescribe the appropriate instruction to help meet those specific needs.

Taking the Final Step

We have taken the first two essential steps in Total Instructional Alignment. We began by organizing curriculum objectives and benchmarks into a logical order using the congruence matrix. Our next step was to analyze the objectives, breaking them down to address both the thinking level required and the sequence of learning required to master each objective. We have one more step to take: regular and effective assessment that provides both students and educators with feedback on students' learning progress. If that feedback is to be successful in affecting student performance on high-stakes assessments, it must also be aligned to the curriculum and instructional strategies as well as to the high-stakes tests themselves. The role of classroom assessment in achieving Total Instructional Alignment is the topic of chapter 5.

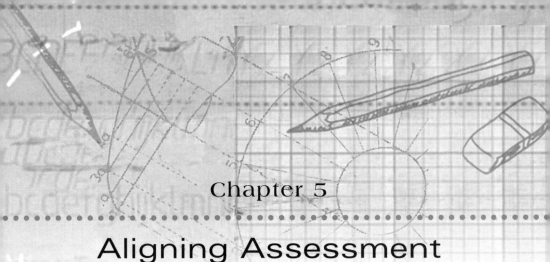

Chapter 5

Aligning Assessment

How do teachers determine that students have learned those things we expect them to learn? Assessment plays a critical role in the Total Instructional Alignment process because it helps us determine what essential learning students have mastered and where they need to go next in the learning process. All too often, assessment results are reviewed briefly and then condemned to a filing cabinet. This data, however, can provide valuable information about student progress and the effectiveness of instruction. It is time that student assessment data comes out of file drawers and into the light of day where it can help students learn.

Two Views of Assessment

It is important to understand that there are actually two ways to view assessment. One view is that the primary purpose of assessment is to assist in what is known as the "sort and select" mission of the school. Those who embrace this function place a heavy emphasis on using test scores to grade, rank, label, and track students, sorting them into homogeneous groupings based on test scores. The other view is that the primary purpose of assessment is to help us gain important information about student learning so that we can adjust instruction to meet individual student needs. The Effective Schools research by Lawrence Lezotte and his colleagues shows that highly successful schools view assessment as a tool that allows them to gain valuable information about where students are in the process of learning—not as a tool to sort and select students. This information is used to adjust the instructional program to meet the needs of individual students. In fact, Lezotte identifies "Frequent Monitoring of Student Progress" as one of the seven correlates of effective schools. By definition, "In the effective school student academic progress is measured frequently through a variety of assessment procedures. The results . . . are used to improve individual student performance and also to improve the instructional program" (Lezotte & McKee, 2002, p. 207).

Clearly, the more frequently we assess, the more information we can gain about our students. The first generation of Effective Schools research cited the importance of teachers closely monitoring student progress in the classroom (Lezotte & McKee, 2006). Every classroom teacher should know where every student is in relationship to what they have mastered and what they need to learn next. The second generation of Effective Schools research places an emphasis on working directly with students to assist them in monitoring their own progress as they learn. This gives students ownership of learning, allowing them to recognize the things they have learned well and what they need to learn next (Lezotte & McKee, 2006). One way this can be done is through the use of mastery grading charts to track student learning progress (Figure 5.1).

In a mastery grading chart, essential learning for the instructional unit is listed across the top of the chart. Teachers can use the chart to track student learning, and students can use individual charts to track their own progress. The teacher can even attach suggested home activities that parents can use to support learning at school.

Teachers should use a variety of assessment procedures in the classroom. Obviously, the way we teach should be aligned to the way we assess our students. How we go about assessing our students depends on what it is we want them to learn.

Unit _____ Teacher _____ Student Name	Learning Task 1	Learning Task 2	Learning Task 3	Assessment	Learning Task 4	Learning Task 5		

Figure 5.1: Mastery Grading Chart

Teaching to Mastery

There was once a hunter who bragged about how he had taught his old hunting dog to sing Yankee Doodle. After years of hearing his bragging, his hunting buddies decided to ask to hear the dog sing. The dog's owner obliged by pulling his old dog out of the back of his truck and sitting down next to him. The hunter then commanded his dog to sing. The dog just panted and wagged his tail. The hunter again asked the dog to sing. Still the dog just sat, panted, and wagged his tail. His buddies began to laugh hysterically. They said, "We always knew you never taught that old dog to sing!" To which the dog's owner replied, "I said I taught him; I didn't say he learned it!"

Today it is more important than ever before that students master essential skills. It is no longer enough to simply cover content. Accountability at all levels requires that teachers not only teach, but that students learn as well.

Teaching to mastery is the idea that all students should be given the appropriate time and support needed to master essential skills. If we are truly committed to leaving no child behind, it is essential that we design programs in our schools that meet the individual needs of all students. We know all students do not learn at the same rate and in the same way. Standards-based instruction may require the teacher to be prepared to re-teach a lesson in a new or different way if a student fails to learn it the first time. Through formative assessment (what Rick Stiggins calls "assessment *for* learning"), the teacher can gain valuable information about what must be re-taught and what the student has mastered well. The teacher may analyze these formative assessments to group students into flexible skill groups for work on areas of weakness or perhaps to enrich areas of strength.

Teachers must also be prepared to determine what they will accept as a standard for mastery. Since this determination can often be very subjective, this standard may vary from teacher to teacher.

What is considered mastery in one classroom may not be mastery in the room next door. To rectify this situation, teachers may come together by grade level or content area and agree on a standard of mastery for a specific skill across a grade level. Some school districts design benchmarking tests to be administered on a quarterly basis. Without these assessments, expectations for mastery tend to vary from school to school. These benchmarking exams set a standard for mastery across the district, creating a level field for all students in all schools within the district.

Regardless of whether the assessments are developed by the individual classroom teacher, a group of grade-level teachers teaching the same content area, or at the district level, the question remains the same: "What will we accept as evidence that students have mastered what we expect them to learn?" These standards of mastery should be rigorous and aligned to state standards and assessments. In order to do this, the teacher must first create an appropriate assessment instrument designed to measure what students are expected to learn.

Types of Assessment

There are two general types of assessment: *criterion referenced* and *norm referenced*. Criterion-referenced tests are tests that are administered to measure predetermined criteria. For example, the Department of Motor Vehicles in every state administers a criterion-referenced test to potential drivers to determine if they are proficient enough to be issued a driver's license. If the potential driver writes the Department of Motor Vehicles and requests it, the department will gladly send a booklet containing everything a safe driver should know and be able to do to drive in that particular state. Similarly, in school, the teacher knows the criteria that will be measured prior to instruction. The assessment measures if the student has mastered the criteria that have been set forth. Most states administer a criterion-referenced test to students at specific grade levels to determine if they have mastered state standards. Keeping with the driver's license analogy, not all the information in the booklet is covered on the actual driver's license exam. This would be far too time-consuming. Rather, the exam is a sampling of questions about the predetermined criteria. In much the same way, most schools administer criterion-referenced assessments that are designed to sample student achievement to see if students have mastered the predetermined standards they are expected to meet.

Many states and local districts still choose to administer a national norm-referenced test to their students. Unlike criterion-referenced tests, these assessments are not written to measure any particular state standards, benchmarks, or learning expectations. The purpose of norm-referenced tests is to determine how a student compares to other students who are taking the same test. Therefore, norm-referenced tests may measure essential skills that are not in the curriculum. As we discussed previously, the congruence matrix is a valuable tool designed to help determine what skills are in the curriculum and what skills are assessed. Usually, state testing programs are designed to measure where students are at the end of a year, or a span of years, in relationship to their learning progress. This is known as summative testing. In order to help students perform well on these assessments, it is important that teachers use frequent classroom assessment to ensure that students are meeting learning goals. It is simply too late to wait to find out at the end of the year.

Classroom Assessment

There are many different forms of classroom or teacher-created assessment that can be used to gain valuable information about students, ranging from the informal to the formal. As an analogy, if we are not feeling well and visit the doctor, he or she may informally assess our health by asking a few questions, checking our temperature, and simply making an educated guess about what is wrong. If we do not get better, we return for a more formal assessment, usually in the form of tests.

Informal Assessment

In the classroom, informal assessment may take the form of watching, listening, and observing students as they work. Another informal assessment may simply be asking the students questions about what they are learning. Their answers can provide the teacher with important information. Most classroom teachers do informal assessment on a daily basis. The strength of this type of assessment is that it is quick and easy to do. There are no papers to grade or essays to read. One drawback of this informal assessment is that what a teacher may find out during observation and student questioning is not always documented. Also, observation without a predetermined rubric may result in a more subjective judgment on behalf of the teacher. Later, a teacher may need a more accurate record of formal data to make summative judgments about a student's learning progress. The observation—"I know Johnny can do it because I saw him do it last Wednesday"—may not be enough. Another consideration is that informal assessment may not always give us quite as accurate a picture of what students know and are able to do as formal assessments do.

Formal Assessment

Just as the doctor orders formal tests to get more accurate information, the classroom teacher may choose to formally assess students on a regular basis to acquire evidence of whether students have mastered essential skills. Since we must be accountable for learning, teachers often rely on the use of formal assessments to gain information about their students.

One type of formal assessment often used by teachers is the paper-and-pencil test. These tests may take the form of true-or-false, matching answers, fill-in-the-blank, multiple choice, open-ended response, or essay-question tests. Paper-and-pencil assessments can give us important information about what students know and are able to do and are frequently used in the classroom to measure student progress.

It is important to ensure that there is congruency between assessment and exactly what we want to know about our students' learning. For example, true-or-false questions are easy to write and easy to score, but there is always a chance that a correct answer was simply a guess. Many true-or-false tests are constructed in such a way that they can only measure basic knowledge. If we want to measure students' ability to think at higher levels, another form of assessment may be more appropriate. Matching and fill-in-the-blank questions usually are designed to measure lower-level thinking skills. When properly designed, however, multiple-choice tests, open-ended questions, and essay tests are excellent ways to assess higher-level thinking skills. Multiple choice assessments are quick and easy to score. Many states use this format as their primary form of testing on state assessments. Open-ended response and essay assessments can provide the teacher with valuable information as well. However, they take time to read and score against a predetermined rubric.

Another type of assessment in the classroom involves the student actually demonstrating proficiency through some kind of performance. An obvious example of performance/demonstration assessment is in physical education class. A student learning to play basketball may have to show that he or she has mastered dribbling the ball, making a free throw, and so on. This is best measured by having the student actually demonstrate the skill. However, the teacher may choose to assess the students' knowledge and understanding of the rules of the game through a paper-and-pencil exam. Another example of performance/demonstration assessment is the high-school biology teacher who assesses students' ability to use a microscope effectively by requiring students to make a slide, properly place and light it, focus the instrument, and so on.

Performance/demonstration assessments require that the teacher establish a predetermined rubric through which to measure student success. Students should be aware of this rubric before they are assessed. An extra benefit of this type of assessment is that it enables students to gain confidence presenting in front of other people.

Another form of demonstration assessment involves group and individual projects. Students may demonstrate they have mastered certain skills by working on a project that requires them to draw on specific knowledge and skills. For example, in fourth-grade science an individual student might create a chart or poster to demonstrate that he or she has mastered the concept of life cycles. Or a group of high-school physics students might collaborate on designing a bridge, demonstrating their ability to integrate and apply principles of physics and math. The teacher then assesses student work through a predetermined rubric that specifies in detail what characterizes excellent, proficient, or substandard levels of mastery. Team efforts on projects such as this have the added bonus of promoting cooperation and collaboration among students, two very important life skills.

Oral presentations can also be used to assess student mastery. These can be done individually or as a team. As with any kind of demonstration assessment, a predetermined scoring rubric must be established by the teacher and made clear to students so they understand the crucial skills necessary for the presentation. Care should be taken to ensure that the skills and content characteristics in the rubric are congruent to the learning standards and process skills reflected in the curriculum and in high-stakes assessments.

Many teachers choose to use portfolio assessment as a means of tracking individual progress toward meeting learning goals. Portfolios are an excellent method to show student growth over a period of time. Allowing students to choose examples of their best work helps them to gain confidence and to see their own growth and improvement. Standardized rubrics that can be applied to several pieces of student work across time permit consistent assessment feedback for both student and teacher. While such rubrics can be more challenging to design than assignment-specific rubrics, the consistency they lend distinguishes real portfolio assessment from just another folder full of student work.

Using film or audio recording to capture student performances allows the teacher to create a kind of portfolio of demonstration assessments. For example, a teacher might audio tape first graders reading simple sentences at the beginning of the year, more complex passages mid-year, and an entire story of their choice by the end of the school year. Filming presentations or having students submit a filmed presentation serves a similar purpose. However, avoid the trap of utilizing film and audio for the sake of simply using this technology; it can be easy to let the technological and administrative requirements of these projects overwhelm their value as assessments. Once again, beginning with a solid rubric will help keep the focus on assessing student learning.

The kind of early learning skills emphasized at primary levels can be challenging to assess. Teachers sometimes choose to keep anecdotal records on students as a means of assessment. The kindergarten teacher might carry a note card to record when he or she sees students demonstrating certain skills during playtime. The skill, time, and date is noted and placed in the child's learning record.

This list only scratches the surface of the many types of classroom assessments teachers use to provide ongoing feedback about student progress. No single assessment technique will be appropriate for every kind of skill and learning, and some creativity is necessary to design assessments that provide fun, engaging learning experiences as well as reliable student performance data. But this kind of ongoing assessment makes the teacher an active researcher in the classroom, as the search for useful information about student achievement replaces habit and guesswork. It will add a new level of professionalism and effectiveness to old teaching practices, and teachers will no longer spend the school year dreading the release of annual test scores. Instead, teachers will know what their students have learned.

Benchmark Testing

Some schools and districts choose to use benchmark assessments with their students at the end of each 9 weeks. Many districts find that without these assessments, expectations for mastery vary from school to school. They may even vary from teacher to teacher within the same school. In other words, what is considered to be an A-level performance in one classroom could very well be considered a C-level performance in the classroom next door. This was the case in an inner-city elementary school where I was principal.

Most of the students in the school came from poor and disadvantaged homes. I remember one fifth-grade student who seemed to try very hard in class. Academically, he was one of the top students and consistently earned straight A's each marking period on his report card. After the second 9 weeks, I was saddened to learn he was moving out of our school district to another district in our school system. I was happy to hear, however, that he would be attending a wonderful new school in a very prominent area of our community. The principal of this new school was a close friend of mine. I called him and asked him to place this student with one of his very best teachers to ensure his continued success. At the end of the third 9 weeks, I called the school to see how the student had done on his report card. Much to my dismay, I was told by my colleague that he had earned four Cs and two Bs. I exclaimed, "That can't be right! He was always a straight-A student at this school." My colleague replied, "Well, he is an average student in this school." This situation exposes the subjectivity of the grading process: Our expectations of A work were not equal to their expectations of A work.

In Total Instructional Alignment, benchmark testing district-wide serves to level the academic playing field for students. In order to do benchmark assessment district-wide, teachers must agree to follow an order of instruction for 9 weeks. Based on that order of instruction, the district develops a rigorous assessment, usually in the same format as the end-of-grade or end-of-course state assessment. This quarterly assessment is designed to measure the essential learning taught during the designated 9-week period. Figure 5.2 shows the essential learning students are to master in each 9-week period in fourth-grade reading.

The first benchmarking exam measures the essential learning from the first 9-week period. The second benchmark exam measures

First 9 Weeks	Second 9 Weeks	Third 9 Weeks	Fourth 9 Weeks
Genre: Poetry	Genre: Fiction	Genre: Nonfiction	Genre: Plays
Reading One-Page Passages	Reading Two-Page Passages	Reading Three-Page Passages	Reading Four-Page Passages
Basic Understanding	Making Generalizations	Analyzing Text	Suffixes
Figurative Language	Story Structure	Skimming Text for Information	Scanning Text for Information
Main Idea	Compare/ Contrast	Cause and Effect Relationships	Venn Diagrams
Predicting Outcomes	Making Inferences	Antonyms	Homonyms
Fact and Opinion	Relating Self to Text	Identifying Relevant Details	Drawing Conclusions
Author's Viewpoint	Summarizing	Prefixes	Relating Text to Text
Drawing Conclusions	Glossary/ Dictionary Skills	Synonyms	Patterns of Organization
KWL Charts	Word Webs	Spider Maps	Review
Benchmark Assessment 1	**Benchmark Assessment 2**	**Benchmark Assessment 3**	**State Assessment 4**

Figure 5.2: Benchmark Testing for Grade Four Reading

the essential learning from the second 9-week period and perhaps spirals back and samples some of the essential learning from the first 9-week period as a review. Likewise, the third 9-week benchmark exam measures all essential learning from the third 9-week period and samples items from the first and second 9-week periods of instruction. The fourth assessment would actually be the state assessment. These benchmark exams can be developed easily from test item banks, or by using old released items from state assessments. If the benchmark exams are administered on scanner sheets and the technology exists within the school, principals and teachers can receive the results of the benchmark exam almost immediately after it is administered. Often, principals and teachers can obtain summaries of how each class and grade level performed as well as a skill-by-skill analysis for each individual student. These results can be used immediately for correction and enrichment.

There is a great deal of benefit derived from benchmark testing students on a regular basis. Not only does a district-wide benchmark test assist in leveling expectations for mastery across the district, but it gives principals and teachers three important opportunities to stop and formally assess where their students are in the mastery of essential skills. Teachers gain information about their teaching by analyzing the results and receive specific remediation and enrichment information concerning their students. Finally, quarterly testing gives students three chances to practice in a testing situation that simulates the actual end-of-grade assessment.

Teaching Test-Taking Skills

Many things can happen when students are not properly prepared to take assessments. Years ago, I recall a charming student named Harry who once refused to take the California Achievement Test. Not only did he refuse to answer the questions, he actually ripped apart his test booklet in complete frustration and threw it to the floor! When I asked the youngster why he was so determined not to take the test, he told me it was because he did not think it was fair. Puzzled, I asked him why he thought the California Achievement Test was unfair. He quickly exclaimed, "Because I have never been to California!"

Fortunately for Harry, this happened at a time when very few assessments held high stakes for students. Today, Harry's refusal might cost him his chance to get to the next grade level. Too many students today still find the format and experience of high-stakes testing as confusing and intimidating as Harry did. Providing students with the test-taking skills they need to demonstrate what they know on these crucial examinations is an important part of the Total Instructional Alignment process.

An entire year of effort put forth by both students and teachers may not be demonstrated if students struggle during the testing situation. If the student gets stuck on the second problem and fails to move on during a timed test, no one will ever know whether he could have answered the questions he missed when time ran out. If a student assumes she knows the directions and does not read them, she may proceed to answer all questions the wrong way. Problems such as these frustrate both students and teachers. It is wrong to assess students on something they have not been taught, and this applies to test format as well as content. It is important to help students learn why tests are important and develop skills that will enable them to do their very best when they are taking tests.

In order for students to "show what they know," they must be adequately prepared with test-taking skills. Teachers find it both relatively easy and extremely beneficial to integrate test-taking skills into their regular instructional program. In particular, students benefit from special attention to understanding test formats, vocabulary development, and increasing their stress-management skills.

Test formats. To be successful at taking standardized tests, students must be able to follow multi-step directions, given either orally or in writing. They must be able to pace themselves and budget their time appropriately. Spending too much time struggling with one question could cause them to miss other questions if time runs out. It is important that students learn to work under pressure. Through practice, students can become accustomed to the pace at which they will have to work to complete the test, and they will learn to recognize when they are spending too much time on any one item. Teachers can help students practice this skill easily during regular instruction in the classroom by using an egg timer to time activities. Other test-taking skills may involve the students' ability to organize their thoughts, transfer answers to a scanner sheet, and recognize common testing signs and symbols. Maintaining concentration over long periods of time is another important test-taking skill. Just keeping two sharpened pencils balanced on their desktop is a major feat for some students! We know that these test-taking skills and others like them cannot be taught a week before the test. They must be a part of the regular instructional program from the beginning of the school year if students are to be successful.

Vocabulary. For students to do their best on standardized assessments, they must possess a large reading vocabulary or, in the case of very young students, a large sight vocabulary. In other words, they must know the meaning of many words and not simply be able to decode the words. This is extremely important because it is not possible to know what words will appear on the assessment. For example, I once observed a student as he was being administered an intelligence test. One analogy question asked, "Nut is to shell as pea is to _____?" I watched in amazement as this bright fifth grader answered the question, "leaf." Later that day, I asked him why he had not responded, "Nut is to shell as pea is to pod."

The fifth grader looked at me with a puzzled expression and said, "Why would you put a pea in a school building?" This student's only experience with pods was at his school where classes were set up in buildings called "pods." This student had heard the principal daily calling for the various pods to report to the cafeteria. This inner-city child had absolutely no experience shelling peas. In this instance, it was not that the student was unable to draw analogies. The problem was simply his lack of the necessary vocabulary.

Stress management. To be successful, students must also be able to control the stress that often accompanies taking tests. Stress can be controlled through proper diet, rest, and exercise. Teachers can make sure students eat a nutritious meal before the assessment, either at school or at home (sending notes home to parents the day before the assessment is one strategy). Teachers may help students relax by having them exercise next to their desks with gentle bending and stretching. Teachers can also help students alleviate stress through relaxation techniques such as deep breathing exercises and listening to quiet, calming music. Another way to relieve stress is by allowing students to use visualization techniques such as closing their eyes and imagining they are in a peaceful environment where they feel totally calm and relaxed.

However, one of the most important ways for both students and teachers to control stress and anxiety is feeling confident and well-prepared for the assessment. Teachers can offer reassurance to students that they have worked hard and are prepared for the testing experience. Usually, the more prepared we feel for a situation, the less stress we experience.

Making It Happen

Clearly, assessment plays a crucial role in the Total Instructional Alignment process. Aligned classroom assessment helps students and teachers focus their energy on the learning students must master so they can perform well on high-stakes assessments. Frequent assessment of student learning provides the teacher with valuable information that can be used to adjust instruction for individual students and to improve the overall school program. End-of-year assessments provide the teacher with important information about how well students have mastered the essential skills throughout the year. Waiting until the end of the year, however, is too late. Teachers must create interim assessments to determine student progress on key knowledge, skills, and concepts throughout the year. These formative tests take on many different formats, depending on what is being taught. Whether employing pencil-and-paper exams or more authentic assessments such as demonstration of skills, teachers are able to use the information to adjust the program for students.

Now that we have traced the process of Total Instructional Alignment from the onset of standards to student success, it is time to address some important questions: How do we make all this happen? How do we maintain student growth and success across many years? What kind of support and leadership is necessary to ensure student success? The final chapter is devoted to the indispensable ingredient in successful implementation of Total Instructional Alignment: leadership.

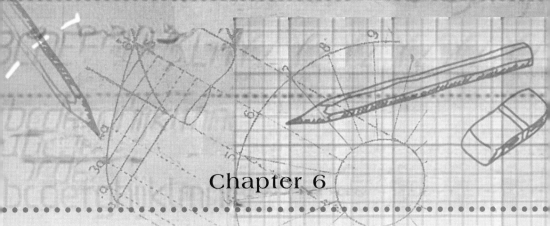

Chapter 6

Leadership and Change

Educators who have been around for a while know that change is constant in education. While some of these changes have been positive, many of them have been practically meaningless. As a result, some teachers have come to view new educational initiatives with caution and skepticism. Often, initiatives are seen as just "this year's new thing." As a result, educators often suffer from what I refer to as TTSP ("This too shall pass") syndrome. Instead of becoming engaged in the initiative, these educators choose to step back and wait out the change. To be successful, Total Instructional Alignment cannot become another flavor of the month. It is a meaningful change with proven success that will truly make a difference and positively impact student learning.

As school leaders know, positive, lasting change does not happen by chance. Someone has to provide the vision, the direction, and the energy to keep the boat from slipping back to the same old course. Leadership is the key to successful implementation of the Total Instructional Alignment process.

The Total Instructional Alignment process can be successfully implemented with the strong leadership of building-level administrators as they work collaboratively with key teacher leaders to plan, organize, and implement the process. Implementation may require changes to policy and procedures, budgeting, professional development, and other core functions within the school. Principals have the authority to make key decisions that can directly impact Total Instructional Alignment at the building level. Success will require shared vision, teamwork, and persistence. Without dedicated leadership, the process is likely to break down and the school will revert back to business as usual. This does not mean that principals must be tyrants or slick sales people. Indeed, just the opposite is true: The key to the process is participatory management. When teachers understand the importance of Total Instructional Alignment and have the knowledge and tools they need to implement it in their classrooms, they will do the right thing. The goal is for teachers to align instruction because they want to, not because they have to. Ironically, this kind of consensus-building is a hallmark of a strong leader.

The Role of the Principal

While leadership should be shared throughout a school's faculty, the role of the principal is simply irreplaceable. No other staff member has the same ability to influence budgets, resources, schedules, and teachers. It is a role that cannot be delegated. A principal's active participation is often the most important factor in determining whether Total Instructional Alignment will be implemented successfully. There are several ways the principal takes Total Instructional Alignment, or any successful school improvement initiative, from idea to implementation so it becomes an accepted part of the school culture. The principal must lead the staff by:

- Always focusing on the initiative

- Helping implement the process

- Always allowing easy access to information and resources

- Monitoring progress

- Inspiring motivation

Focusing on the Initiative

Once, many years ago, I learned a lesson about the power of focus. I had a cat that did not particularly like visits to the veterinarian. On one dreaded trip, she needed a shot. I asked the veterinarian if I could leave the room because I knew it would be disastrous. The veterinarian assured me that the cat would be fine and would not even know she was getting the shot. I watched in amazement as he began to slide her across the table. Nervous about the possibility of falling off, the cat intently watched where she was going. The cat did not make a sound or even blink when the veterinarian gave her the shot. She was too focused on sliding off the table!

This is the kind of single-minded focus principals need as they implement Total Instructional Alignment. Not only must principals keep themselves focused on the alignment process, they must keep their faculties, students, and the entire school community focused on the school's academic achievement goals as well. The principal must ensure that all school functions that affect instruction, such as remedial programs and tutoring opportunities, are aligned with the process. Making Total Instructional Alignment a primary instructional focus will help alleviate some of the day-to-day distractions that do not contribute to quality instruction and successful student learning (such as meaningless busy work or time-consuming programs that have little to do with the teaching or learning process).

Principals should begin by communicating the importance of the Total Instructional Alignment process to teachers. I have found that, for the most part, what the principal believes to be important, the teachers believe to be important. Key elements of the process must be built into daily activities, staff meetings, and grade- or subject-level planning sessions. In such areas as scheduling, budgeting, and staff assignments, the key question should always be, "How will this decision enhance our students' ability to meet learning standards?" In all communications, both formal and informal, the teaching task should be framed in terms of Total Instructional Alignment.

Implementing the Process

Another way principals support the Total Instructional Alignment process is by playing a formative role in its implementation. Providing teachers with the necessary knowledge and tools through quality professional development experiences is critical. The other essential resource the principal must provide is time—the necessary time for teachers to meet and plan together. A wise superintendent once told me, "You can't find time because it was never lost, and you can't create time because you weren't given the gift. All you can do is take a critical look at the time you are given and use it very wisely." The key is to reallocate the time we have been given. Usually, people can find time for things they believe to be important. Using faculty staff meetings, grade-level and vertical team planning sessions, and teacher planning days to promote the Total Instructional Alignment process is a wise use of time.

Allowing Easy Access to Information and Resources

Once, in a training session, I was holding up a curriculum document as I was describing something to a group of teachers. One teacher raised her hand and asked what the document was. I explained that it was their district-level curriculum guide. She gasped and said she had never seen it before. I found out later that she returned to school to investigate. The documents were finally located locked away in an old bathroom that was being used for storage. The box the curriculum guide came in had never even been opened!

It is all too easy for information to get lost like this, whether it is hidden away in an unused lavatory or a drawer in the principal's office. Unused information is worse than useless information; it is positively counterproductive to performance improvement efforts. Therefore, one of the chief responsibilities of the principal is to evaluate the circulation of information within the building to promote the success of the Total Instructional Alignment process. It is important for the principal to ensure that all teachers have easy access to the information they need to align instruction in their classrooms. This information may be in the form of data reports, curriculum documents, and individual classroom curriculum maps, lesson plans, and assessment and progress reports. Teachers should have easy access to all relevant standards documents, curriculum guides, and assessment information. The assessment data should be in an understandable format and disaggregated as needed. Especially useful are data results over multiple years that allow teachers to look at patterns and trends in student learning and growth over time. In addition, it is the responsibility of the principal to ensure that accurate and appropriate inter- and intra-school comparisons are drawn from the data. Keep in mind that the primary purpose of testing students is to improve learning—not to rate and rank teachers.

Monitoring Progress

Monitoring progress is another crucial role the principal plays in the Total Instructional Alignment process. Obviously, things that are regularly checked tend to get done. Although the Total Instructional Alignment process should be the basis for formal reviews and evaluation of teacher effectiveness, it should also be a part of informal classroom walkthrough visits. In order to monitor adequately, principals should spend time in classrooms daily. The Total Instructional Alignment process cannot be effectively monitored from the front office. This does not mean that principals have to spend an hour in each classroom every day. For most principals, this would not even be possible. On the contrary, when principals know what to look for they can very quickly become aware of how well the process is occurring when they visit classrooms.

There are four important instructional criteria the principal should look for during classroom visits:

- Standards-based/objective-based instruction
- Congruency
- A diagnostic-prescriptive approach
- Frequent monitoring of student learning

Standards-based/objective-based instruction. Principals should look for evidence that the teacher has established clear goals for each lesson that link to standards and curriculum. I remember the first lesson observation and feedback conference I held with a classroom teacher when I was a new principal. When she entered my office, I asked her if she would like a cup of coffee. While I was leaving my office to retrieve her coffee, I casually asked her to open the standards document on the table and identify the learning goal for the lesson I just observed. When I came back in the room, she was still flipping pages and looked somewhat embarrassed. She did not know which, if any, standard the lesson addressed. The lesson was just an activity she had done with her students for years. I assured her that it was not a problem to go above and beyond the essential content we expect students to learn. What is important is that we do not do this at the expense of the essential content.

Congruency. The second criterion is congruency to the learning goal. Does the information presented in the lesson align with the learning goal? Do questions and learning activities provided during the lesson move students toward the goal? Listening to the verbs the teacher uses in questions and activities can help determine the complexity of thinking involved during instruction. For example, if the teacher asks students to compare two forms of government for likenesses and differences, the verb "compare" signals that the question or activity engages students at the analysis level of thinking.

A diagnostic/prescriptive approach. The third criterion principals should look for is a diagnostic/prescriptive approach to instruction. That is, the teacher's focus with the entire class and with each individual student should be driven by identified learning needs. Simply because a learning goal is in the curriculum guide or standards document does not mean it needs to be taught. It may be that some students already know it, while others may not yet possess the requisite skills to learn it. If teachers take time to assess prior knowledge before beginning instruction, they are more likely to ensure that the lesson is at the right level of difficulty for students.

Years ago, I had the opportunity to observe an excellent lesson being taught in a kindergarten classroom. The teacher told the children that by the end of the lesson they would be able to recognize five common farm animals. These animals turned out to be the pig, the chicken, the horse, the rooster, and the cow. As the teacher showed the children each plastic model farm animal, the children were to pick up the appropriate plastic animal on their own tables and repeat the name of the animal back to the teacher. The students cooperated fully and appeared to enjoy holding the plastic animals. The only problem was that this school was in a rural area. Most of the students in the class already knew what she teaching; in fact, some of the children probably had to feed a few of those animals before coming to school that day! When I asked the teacher why she chose to teach that particular lesson, she innocently replied, "Because it was an objective in the curriculum guide." If the teacher had taken time before instruction to assess prior knowledge, she would have discovered that the lesson was unnecessary. She might have decided to increase the difficulty of the learning task or move on to something completely different. In order to align instruction in the classroom, teachers must be diagnostic and prescriptive in their instructional practice.

Frequent monitoring of student learning. Finally, the principal should see evidence that the teacher is frequently monitoring student learning throughout the instructional process. In order to ensure that students are learning, teachers must have strategies to get periodic feedback from all learners to make appropriate decisions about how to proceed in the instructional process. Just as a nurse checks each patient and makes the appropriate adjustments in care based on the patient's condition, a teacher must check where each child is in the learning process and change the instruction as needed. Teachers can do this by moving around the classroom and observing students as they work. Teachers can also listen to student discussions or ask them to signal responses to questions. Knowing where each student is during instruction allows the teacher to make the mid-course adjustments in instruction that are necessary to ensure that all students are learning.

As the principal uses these four criteria to observe and communicate with teachers about the Total Instructional Alignment process in the classroom, a powerful common language will begin to emerge. This common language provides a structure that allows teachers and administrators to communicate quickly and freely about instruction and student learning.

Inspiring Motivation

Principals who manage change successfully understand the power of motivation. Communicating a clear and consistent vision about the Total Instructional Alignment process and its importance to student learning is key to this role. This vision must be shared with all the stakeholders: faculty, students, parents, and the community. To perform this role, principals must become extremely familiar with performance data and goals.

As the school moves forward in the process, effective leaders find ways to recognize and celebrate success whenever they can. As a principal, I once found myself eating my lunch on the roof of the school. That was the way students had chosen to celebrate improvement and gains in end-of-year test scores. The superintendent climbed up the ladder and joined me for pizza that was delivered to us personally by the president of the Parent-Teacher Association.

Unfortunately, we do not always meet with success during the process of change. Sometimes we encounter setbacks. As motivator, the principal finds ways to use these setbacks as an opportunity to reapply and reinforce Total Instructional Alignment methods. It is important that we view problems as opportunities to learn more about the process and to improve. The principal must intervene with educators to ensure they are aware that data arising from this process will be their consistent performance feedback. The rewards from the Total Instructional Alignment process will be positive for both teachers and students. Since we know what can happen to students when instruction is not aligned, it must be clear to everyone that refusal to participate in the process is not an option.

Building Faculty Leadership

Despite the crucial nature of the principal's leadership role, Effective Schools research recognizes that the principal is truly a leader of leaders when it comes to instruction (Lezotte & McKee, 2002). Leadership density (not to be confused with dense leadership!) is an important part of the Total Instructional Alignment process. Although the principal may be the top administrator at the building level, he or she cannot do the job alone. Even the most energetic and enthusiastic leader cannot carry the entire weight of the process. Total Instructional Alignment is not simply an application of techniques; it is a transformative way of thinking about education, one that leads to changes in the hearts and minds of teachers. In order for this to occur, teachers must own the process, and to own it they must feel a sense of participation at some level.

Fortunately, the Total Instructional Alignment process has many built-in opportunities for teacher leadership. Teachers can be involved in constructing and analyzing congruence matrices, analyzing vertical alignment, developing common classroom assessments, and analyzing performance data. In grade-level, subject-area, or vertical teams, there are many opportunities for teachers to lead one portion of the process or another. Teachers can also help monitor the process in the building and assist in the design of mid-course corrections if they are needed. Teacher-leaders can be invaluable to the principal when they assist in the development and presentation of professional development. The more teacher-leaders assist in leading the process, the greater the chance it will meet with success. Active involvement in the leadership process motivates the teacher, increases his or her own understanding of the process, and decreases any temptation to maintain a skeptical distance.

Taking the First Step

My first principalship was in an inner-city school. The students in this school came from four housing projects located just blocks away. Ninety-eight percent of the students were minority kids from very poor and disadvantaged situations. The students were bright and for the most part seemed to enjoy being at school each day. The teachers in this school had good hearts and worked hard. The results of their efforts, however, were simply invisible each year at testing time. Students scored well below average, year after year. As a result, many teachers became disillusioned and began to accept— and even expect—these below-average test scores. Frustrated and ready for change, I attended a presentation to learn more about the process of becoming an effective school. There had to be something we could do to improve our students' success.

Dr. Lawrence Lezotte, the now-famous proponent of the Effective Schools movement, was the keynote speaker. During the presentation, he spoke of a school that sounded very similar to ours. Most of the students who attended this school were minority students living in poverty. The school was situated in a drug-infested neighborhood where there was literally shooting in the streets. It sounded a lot like our school.

Dr. Lezotte asked an important question that completely changed my way of thinking: How many people in the audience, which was made up of teachers and administrators, believed that the average test score in the school he described was below the fiftieth percentile? Almost every hand went up. Then he asked how many believed it was below the fortieth percentile. Still hands went up. He had not told us one thing about the school itself—not about the teachers, the principal, or the curriculum. Everything he had described was about the circumstances from which the children had come, circumstances that were for the most part beyond the control of the school or the children. Still, most people had already formed opinions about the students in that school.

After a pause, Dr. Lezotte told us that the average test score in the school was above the 90th percentile. A hush fell over the room. Our average test score on the same assessment was below the 30th percentile.

Later that afternoon, I thought about what I had heard. When I returned to school, I found the telephone number for the school Dr. Lezotte spoke of and I arranged a visit. Six months later, a handful of teachers and I took the 7-hour road trip to Maryland. We spent a day visiting the school. We sat in classrooms and watched teachers teach and students learn. We talked with the principal, teachers, students, and parents about the educational program offered there. We looked at testing data and discussed how the faculty used the data to improve instruction. We were confronted with the fact that students like ours, in a school like ours, could achieve excellence.

Late that afternoon we began the trip home. Sitting in the driver's seat, I certainly had plenty to think about on that long drive. Then I heard the windows of the van going up and down. The teachers were throwing their excuses out the window. One teacher commented, "Did you hear the last one go out? That was the one about how our students do not do well on assessments because they come from poor and disadvantaged homes. We surely can't use that one anymore!" Maybe the long hours on the road and the excitement of what we had seen made them a little light-headed, but they had invented their own ritual for disposing of the excuses we had for so long accepted for poor student learning results.

That is how we began our journey toward becoming an effective school through the process of Total Instructional Alignment, and our students have reaped the positive results of our efforts. Today, I often tell people that if they ever drive between Maryland and North Carolina down Interstate 95, they should keep an eye out for our discarded excuses, because that is where we left them.

Total Instructional Alignment is designed to provide educators with a common-sense approach to the alignment process based on what we know about quality instruction and the principles and practices of effective schools. It continues to evolve through my work with thousands of teachers and administrators across the country as they strive to find meaningful and creative ways to make TIA a reality in their classrooms, schools, and districts.

The ultimate goal of Total Instructional Alignment is student learning success. It requires effort and work, but it can be done if teachers and principals are equipped with courage, knowledge, and skills. It makes sense that students tend to learn those things they are taught. If we truly believe all students can learn given the time and resources necessary, we must do everything in our power to ensure that it happens in every classroom.

References and Additional Resources

Abbott, S. (1997). *Standardized testing*. Westminster, CA: Teacher Created Materials, Inc.

Block, P. (1991). *The empowered manager*. San Francisco: Jossey-Bass.

Block, P. (1993). *Stewardship*. San Francisco: Berrett-Koehler Publishers.

Bloom, B. S. (1976). *Human characteristics and school learning.* New York: McGraw Hill.

Brookover, W. B. (1996). *Creating effective schools* (Rev. ed.). Holmes Beach, FL: Learning Publications.

Carroll, J. B. (1963). A model for school learning. *Teachers College Record, 64,* 723–733.

Covey, S. (1990). *The 7 habits of highly effective people.* New York: Free Press.

Covey, S. (1992). *Principle centered leadership.* New York: Simon & Schuster.

Covey, S. (1994). *First things first.* New York: Simon & Schuster.

Cummings, C. (1990). *Teaching makes a difference.* Edmond, WA: Teaching, Inc.

Cummings, C. (1996). *Managing to teach* (2nd ed.). Edmond, WA: Teaching, Inc.

Deming, W. E. (1982). Out of crisis. Cambridge: Massachusetts Institute of Technology.

Dolan, W. P. (1994). *Restructuring our schools: A primer on systemic change.* Kansas City: Systems & Organization.

Economic Research Service. (2000, September). *A history of American agriculture, 1607–2000.* (ERS-POST-12.) Washington, DC: Author.

Flippo, R. (1988). *Testwise: Strategies for success in taking tests.* Belmont, CA: Fearon Teacher Aids.

Fullan, M. G. (1991). *The new meaning of educational change.* New York: Teachers College Press.

Gagne, R. M. (1987). *Instructional technology: Foundations.* Hillsdale, NJ: Lawrence Erlbaum Associates, Inc.

Gentile, J. R. (1988). *Instructional improvement: Summary and analysis of Madeline Hunter's essential elements of instruction and supervision.* Oxford, OH: National Staff Development Council.

Guskey, T. (1985). *Implementing mastery learning in the classroom.* Belmont, CA: Wadsworth.

Hunter, M. (1982). *Mastery teaching.* El Segundo, CA: TIP Publications.

Hunter, M. (1989). Madeline Hunter in the English classroom. *English Journal, 78*(5), 16–18.

Hunter, M., & Russell, D. (1990). *Mastering coaching and supervision.* El Segundo, CA: TIP Publications.

Hutchins, R. M. (1972). *Conflict in education in a democratic society.* Westport, CN: Greenwood Publishers Group.

Jacobson, J., Olsen, C., Rice, J. K., Sweetland, S., & Ralph, J. (2001). *Educational achievement and black-white inequality.* Washington, DC: National Center for Educational Statistics.

Jasmine, J. (1997). *How to prepare your middle school students for standardized tests.* Huntington Beach, CA: Teacher Created Materials.

Lezotte, L. (1991). *Correlates of Effective Schools: The first and second generations.* Okemos, MI: Effective Schools Products, Ltd.

Lezotte, L. (1994). *Essential prerequisites for achieving school reform.* Okemos, MI: Effective Schools Products, Ltd.

Lezotte, L. (1997). *Learning for all: What will it take?* Okemos, MI: Effective Schools Products, Ltd.

Lezotte, L., & Jacoby, B. (1992). *A guide to sustainable school reform: The district context for school improvement.* Okemos, MI: Effective Schools Products, Ltd.

Lezotte, L., & McKee, K. (2002). *Assembly required: A continuous school improvement system.* Okemos, MI: Effective Schools Products, Ltd.

Lezotte, L., & McKee, K. (2006). *Stepping up: Leading the charge to improve our schools.* Okemos, MI: Effective Schools Products, Ltd.

Lezotte, L., & Pepperl, J. (1999). *The Effective Schools process: A proven path to learning for all.* Okemos, MI: Effective Schools Products, Ltd.

National Education Commission on Time and Learning (1994). *Prisoners of time.* Retrieved October 10, 2006, from www.ed.gov/pubs/PrisonersOfTime.

New standards, same old teaching. (2000, February 16). *USA Today.*

Pritchett, P. (1996). *Resistance: Moving beyond the barriers of change.* Plano, TX: Pritchett and Associates.

Senge, P. M. (1990). *The fifth discipline: The art and practice of the learning organization.* New York: Doubleday.

Shedd, J. P., & Bacharach, S. B. (1991). *Tangled hierarchies: Teachers as professionals and the management of schools.* San Francisco: Jossey-Bass.

Stiggins, R. (2005). From formative assessment to assessment FOR learning: A path to success in standards-based schools. *Phi Delta Kappan, 87*(4), 324–328.

Tomlinson, C. A. (1995). *How to differentiate instruction in mixed-ability classrooms.* Alexandria, VA: Association for Supervision and Curriculum Development.

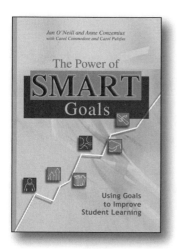

The Power of SMART Goals:
Using Goals to Improve Student Learning
Jan O'Neill and Anne Conzemius with
Carol Commodore and Carol Pulsfus
This easy-to-read guide will help your staff set
effective goals that are Strategic and Specific,
Measurable, Attainable, Results-based and
Time-bound. That's SMART! **BKF207**

Whatever It Takes: How Professional
Learning Communities Respond When Kids
Don't Learn (Audio Book)
Richard DuFour, Rebecca DuFour,
Robert Eaker, and Gayle Karhanek
Transform your commute into a learning oppor-
tunity. This audio book details how professional
learning communities provide struggling students
with additional time and support. **AUF003**

The Handbook for SMART School Teams
Anne Conzemius and Jan O'Neill
Improve processes and systems in your
school as an effective team. This practical
handbook shows you how to build a solid
network of support. **BKF392**

Professional Learning Communities at
Work Plan Book
Rebecca DuFour, Richard DuFour,
and Robert Eaker
With space for eight class periods, this
process book helps teacher teams address
crucial PLC concepts. **BKF217**